ABOUT THE

C000049891

Brian M. Stratton is a successful Department of Transport
Approved Driving Instructor (A.D.I.), teaching
advanced driving and training A.D.I.'s.

Together with personal driving experience of well over half million
miles (spanning 17 years), the author has also achieved the
following very high standards within the Driver Training Industry:

DIAmond Advanced Instructor
(out of 33,000 A.D.I.'s, only 120 are DIAmond Advanced Instructors)

RoSPA Diploma
(A diploma in Advanced Driving Techniques, held by only 180 people)

He has also successfully completed several Rally Driving Courses
and attended a Police Better Driving Course,
including skid-pan training.

Two other widely acclaimed Driving Reference Books, by the same author
are:

A.D.I. Part III: Essential Information

The Driving Test: Graphic Traffic Version

If you have any questions about motoring matters or the driving
test, please contact the publisher: (0860) 260720

ALSO BY THE SAME AUTHOR
ADI PART III : Essential Information
The Test Of Ability To Instruct

A completely new book (published November 1990) on the subject of the
Part III of the ADI Qualifying Exam.

Chapters include:
* Choosing a Trainer
* Recent Changes to the Part III
* How the Part III is Marked
* Using the Question & Answer Technique
* Suggested Introductions and Hints for each Exercise

Ideal for candidates preparing for the Part III, this book is a valuable
complement to any training course.
Information for this book has come from many sources:

* Accompanying candidates on Part III tests
* Discussing the subject with supervising examiners
* Attending ADI trainers' seminars at Cardington
* Listening to candidates' queries regarding the test

For details of availability and price please contact:
First Time (publishers) : Tel (0860) 260720

THE DRIVING TEST : Graphic Traffic Version

ISBN : 0-9514415 - 7 - 4

This book covers all aspects of the Driving Test, and chapters include :

* How the test is marked
* What the examiners look for
* Hints to help you pass first time
* 100 Highway code questions (taken from tests)
* Traffic signs
* ... *PLUS much more* ...

All information is presented in pictorial format. A humorous style makes for
easy reading, helping you to remember vital facts.

Size: 148m x 210mm   A5 Landscape, 120 pages

For more information please contact the publisher on : (0860) 260720

HILL START BLUES

A New Driving Manual for the 1990's

By

Brian M. Stratton

The title HILL START BLUES and the lay-out of this book are copyright
©Brian M. Stratton 1990.

No part of this book may be reproduced, stored in a retrieval system or
transmitted in any form or by any means, electronic, electrostatic, magnetic tape,
mechanical, photocopying, recording or otherwise without permission in writing
from the publisher.

Note: Whilst every effort has been made to ensure the complete accuracy of
this book, neither the author nor publisher can accept liability for any error or
misinterpretation of the information contained herein.

Published by First Time Driving. (0860) 260720

© Copyright Brian M. Stratton 1990

First published in Great Britain in 1990
Revised Edition 1991

The extracts from "Syllabus for Learner Drivers" are reproduced with the permission of the Controller of Her Majesty's Stationery Office

Type setting and diagrams by
Text & Graphics
161-163 Beckenham Road
Beckenham
Kent.

Copyright © Brian M. Stratton 1990

ISBN 0-9514415-6-6

This book is sold subject to the condition that it shall not, by way of trade or otherwise, be lent, re-sold, hired out, or otherwise circulated without the publishers prior consent in any form of binding or cover other than that in which it is published.

CONTENTS

DIAGRAMS

FOREWORD

This book has been designed to be easily read and understood.

It can be read from cover to cover (driving tasks are explained in a logical sequence) or 'dipped' into as necessary.

Each chapter has been sub-divided with sub-headings to make studying easier.

Ideally this book should be used in conjunction with driving lessons you have from an approved driving instructor (A.D.I.). Before your lesson read the specific chapter relating to the content of the lesson. This will give you an excellent theoretical knowledge of the driving tasks and your lesson will enable you to put that knowledge into practice.

NEW SYLLABUS, WHAT NEW SYLLABUS?

INTRODUCTION

Driving is a life skill, and full mastery of the knowledge and skills set out in this syllabus can only be acquired over many years. The syllabus sets out the skills in which every driver should achieve a basic competence in order to pass the L test. The learner driver is strongly recommended to study it.

In addition to this syllabus drivers should have a thorough knowledge of the Highway Code and of the motoring laws.

They should also have a thorough understanding of their responsibilities as drivers. This means a real concern not only for their own safety, but also for the safety of every other road user, including pedestrians.

Most new drivers learn with an Approved Driving Instructor (A.D.I.) - make sure your instructor covers this syllabus fully.

RECOMMENDED SYLLABUS FOR LEARNING TO DRIVE A CAR

1. LEGAL REQUIREMENTS

A learner driver must:-

1.1 be at least 17 years old (except that persons receiving a mobility allowance [for a disability] may start driving a car when 16 years old);

1.2 be able to read in good daylight (with glasses or contact lenses, if worn) a motor vehicle number plate 20.5 metres away with symbols 79.4mm high;

1.3 be medically fit to drive;

1.4 hold a provisional driving licence (or comply with the conditions for holding a provisional licence - see leaflet D100). (D100 is a leaflet containing general information about driver licensing. It is issued free by DVLC Swansea and is available at post offices).

1.5 ensure the vehicle being driven is legally roadworthy, has a current test certificate (if it is over the prescribed age limit) and is properly licensed with the tax disc displayed;

1.6 make sure the use of the vehicle is properly insured;

1.7 display L plates which are visible from the front and the back of the vehicle;

1.8 be accompanied by a supervisor - that is someone who has held a full British licence for 3 years for the kind of vehicle being driven and is at least 21 years of age;

1.9 wear a seat belt unless granted an exemption and see that all seat belts in the vehicle and their anchorages and fittings are free from obvious defects;

1.10 ensure that children under 14 are suitably restrained by an approved child restraint or an adult seat belt;

1.11 be aware that the legal requirement to notify medical conditions which could affect safe driving and, in cases where a vehicle has been adapted for a disability, ensure that the adaptations are suitable to control the vehicle safely;

1.12 know the rules concerning the issue and production of driving licences, insurance certificates and road excise licences, and on the restrictions on learner drivers.

2. CAR CONTROLS, EQUIPMENT AND COMPONENTS

A learner driver should:-

2.1 understand the function of the accelerator, clutch, gears, footbrake and steering and be able to use them competently;

2.2 know and be competent in using other controls and switches in the car that have a bearing on road safety;

2.3 understand the meaning of the gauges or other displays on the instrument panel;

2.4 know the legal requirements for the vehicle;

2.5 be able to carry out routine safety checks that do not require tools and be able to identify possible defects; particularly with regard to the steering system, brakes, tyres, seat belts, lights, reflectors, direction indicators, windscreen wipers and washers, horn, rear view mirrors, speedometer and exhaust system;

2.6 know the safety factors relating to vehicle loading.

3. ROAD USER BEHAVIOUR

A learner driver should:-

3.1 know the most common causes of accidents;

3.2 know which road users are most at risk on the roads and how to reduce that risk;

3.3 know the rules, risks and effects of drinking and driving;

3.4 know the effect of fatigue, illness and drugs on driving performance;

3.5 be aware of age dependent problems among other road users - especially among children, teenagers and the elderly;

3.6 be alert and able to anticipate the likely actions of other road users and be able to suggest appropriate precautions;

3.7 be aware that courtesy and consideration towards other road users are essential qualities for safe driving.

4. VEHICLE CHARACTERISTICS

A learner driver should:-

4.1 know the most important principles concerning braking distances and road-holding under various road and weather conditions;

4.2 know the handling characteristics of other vehicles with regard to typical stability, speed, braking and manoeuvrability;

4.3 know that some vehicles are less easily seen than others;

4.4 be able to assess the risks caused by the characteristics of other vehicles and suggest precautions that can be taken; e.g. large commercial vehicles pulling to the right before turning left; blind areas for drivers of some commercial vehicles and bicycles and motorcycles being buffeted by strong winds.

5. ROAD AND WEATHER CONDITIONS

A learner driver should:-

5.1 know the particular hazards of driving in both daylight and the dark, on different types of roads, e.g. roads that are single carriageway (including country lanes), 3 lane, dual carriageway and motorway;

5.2 gain experience of driving on urban and higher speed roads (but not motorways) in both daylight and darkness;

5.3 know which road surfaces provide the better and poorer grip when braking;

5.4 know the hazards caused by adverse weather conditions, e.g. rain, fog, snow, icy roads and strong cross winds;

5.5 be able to assess the risks caused by road and traffic conditions, be aware of how the conditions may cause others to drive unsafely, and be able to take appropriate precautions.

6. TRAFFIC SIGNS, RULES AND REGULATIONS

A learner driver should:-

6.1 have a sound knowledge of the meaning of traffic signs and road markings;

6.2 have a good grasp of the traffic rules and regulations, e.g. speed limits, parking restrictions, zebra and pelican crossings.

7. CAR CONTROL AND ROAD PROCEDURE

A learner driver should have the knowledge and skill to safely and competently carry out the following tasks, in both daylight and darkness, making proper use of mirrors and signals before manoeuvring, where appropriate:-

7.1 take the necessary precautions before getting in or out of the vehicle;

7.2 carry out the cockpit drill including the fitting of seat belts and take the proper precautions before starting the engine;

7.3 start the engine and move away straight ahead and at an angle on the level and on uphill and downhill gradients;

7.4 select the correct road position for normal driving;

7.5 take proper observation in all traffic situations;

7.6 adjust speed to that suitable for the road and traffic conditions;

7.7 react promptly to risk situations;

7.8 change traffic lanes;

7.9 pass stationary vehicles;

7.10 meet, overtake and cross the path of other vehicles;

7.11 turn right and left at junctions (including crossroads and round-abouts);

7.12 drive ahead at crossroads and roundabouts;

7.13 keep a safe separation gap when following other vehicles;

7.14 act correctly at pedestrian crossings;

7.15 show proper regard for the safety of other road users, with particular care towards the most vulnerable;

7.16 drive on both urban and rural roads and, where possible, dual carriageway - keeping up with the traffic flow where it is safe and proper to do so;

7.17 comply with traffic regulations and traffic signs and signals given by the police, traffic wardens and other road users;

7.18 stop the vehicle safely, normally and in an emergency, without locking the wheels;

7.19 turn the vehicle in the road, to face the opposite way, using the forward and reverse gears;

7.20 reverse the vehicle into a side turning keeping reasonably close to the kerb;

7.21 park parallel to the kerb while driving in reverse gear;

7.22 park the vehicle in multi-storey car parks, or other parking bays, on the level, uphill and downhill, both in forward and in reverse direction;

7.23 cross all types of railway level crossings.

8. ADDITIONAL KNOWLEDGE

A learner driver should know:-

8.1 the importance of correct tyre pressures;

8.2 the action to take to correct skids;

8.3 how to drive through fords and flooded areas;

8.4 what to do if involved in a breakdown or accident including the special arrangements in the case of breakdowns and accidents on motorways;

8.5 basic first aid for use on the road as set out in the Highway Code;

8.6 the action to take to deter car thieves.

9. MOTORWAY DRIVING

Learner drivers should gain a sound knowledge of the special rules, regulations and driving techniques for motorway driving prior to taking their driving test. After passing their test they are advised to take motorway lessons with an A.D.I. before driving unsupervised on motorways.

1992 - CHANGES TO DRIVER TRAINING AND THE DRIVING TEST

During the early 1990's, changes will be made in driver training and the driving test that will harmonise the GB driving test with other EEC member countries.

The time-scale of these changes will be:

* Early 1990 : new syllabus introduced. Learner drivers are advised to study and cover this with a professional driving instructor (A.D.I.)

* April 1991 : Drivers will be expected to be able to perform three manoeuvres (reverse round a corner, turn-in-the-road and a parking exercise). At least two of these manoeuvres must be included in the driving test. In the parking exercise the candidate will be asked to pull up alongside a single parked vehicle and to reverse-park parallel to the kerb within a distance of 1.5 - 2 car lengths. Selection of which two manoeuvres should be performed on each test would be random. Including the option of a parking exercise in the test highlights for novice drivers the importance of parking skills.

* Mid 1991 : Candidates will be expected to have a depth of knowledge over a wider range of subjects:

* Legal requirements for the vehicle.

* How to carry out safety checks.

* How accidents are caused, and what can be done to reduce risks.

* Identifying vehicle defects.

* Effects/risk of drink driving.

* Be aware of vulnerable road users.

* How to drive in adverse weather conditions.

* Night driving.

* What to do in the event of an accident.

* Basic first aid.

* Motorway driving (theory).

* Traffic rules and regulations.

* Traffic signs and road markings.

As a test of theoretical knowledge driving test candidates will be asked a certain number of questions and will be expected to have a thorough knowledge of the highway code and motoring laws, as well as understanding their responsibilities as a driver.

Your professional driving instructor (A.D.I.) should keep himself informed of any impending changes in driver training and should be able to structure tuition so that all subjects are thoroughly covered.

The ultimate aim of these changes is to:

Reduce the number of injuries/deaths from road traffic accidents. 5,000 people are killed each year on the roads. The cause of 95% of these accidents is human error.

Prepare drivers thoroughly by achieving a basic competence in driving skills. Obviously experience will come over many years.

Driver education is therefore vital. If drivers are not taught how to do things correctly and safely by a professional driving instructor, who is going to teach them? Bear in mind that when learning to drive it is very probably the only paid for tuition that you will have for driving, so make the most of it. Accept the advice and help that your A.D.I. gives you and remember that any advice given is in your own best interest, and the interest of other road users.

NOTE: EEC type Driving Licences will be issued to all who pass the Driving Test from April 1st 1990. It will be a two-coloured sheet of paper (which will fold to fit in a clear plastic wallet), a pink part as the licence and a green part for endorsements, and stating what type of vehicles may be driven.

A pink European Community style licence was introduced for new drivers in 1986, but a separate licence was needed for PSV (Public Service Vehicles) and HGV (Heavy Goods Vehicles) drivers. Existing licences will not need to be changed.

7

1

DRIVING LESSONS . . .

HOW TO GET THE MOST OUT OF THEM

1.1 Structured training

The driving lessons that you have from an A.D.I. (Approved Driving Instructor) will generally be the only professional tuition for driving a car that you have. It is therefore important that you make the most of these lessons; after all you are paying for them!

Driving lessons should provide you with structured tuition - this means building your knowledge of driving in stages which lead on logically from each other. Your instructor will explain everything to you in a clear and logical way, and will be prepared to demonstrate any manoeuvre or aspect of driving. If you are unclear about anything he will explain it to you again, in more detail or in a different way if necessary. Even if a question seems trivial do not be afraid to ask!

1.2 Record of progress . . .

The main aims of your driving lessons are:
  (1) to ensure that you are a safe and competent driver, and
  (2) that you pass your driving test.

Within the framework of your lessons your instructor should outline the objectives (attainable targets) for each lesson. This ensures that you know what you will be doing in that lesson; at the end of which your instructor will evaluate your progress, and inform you of the content of the next lesson.

Your instructor should keep a record of your progress. Most instructors will have a minimum of 25 pupils, often more, and without a record of progress it is very difficult to recall each individual's level of driving.

You should be given an appointment card which will tell you when your next lessons will be. Keep this card safe and bring it along with you to all of your lessons.

Driving lessons can vary in length: 45, 50 or 60 minutes. Check when you book your lessons - you may think you are paying for one hour but it may turn out to be 45 minutes.

1.3 Other pupils in the car?

Also check whether other pupils will be in the car - some instructors do this as a means of running one lesson on to another with no 'wasted' time driving between lessons to collect the next pupil.

When thinking about booking driving lessons it is advisable to ask around to see if friends or relatives can recommend a good instructor. When booking a first lesson ask if you will be given structured training with progress reports - if you get a vague or negative response, go elsewhere!

Lessons can be taken in whatever combination you choose; one one-hour lesson per week, one two-hour lesson per week, two one-hour lessons per week, etc. etc. Experience has shown that most learners will gain most benefit from two one-hour lessons per week.

1.4 On your lesson . . .

Ideally a driving lesson should follow a pattern (a 60 minute lesson is assumed here) similar to that shown below. Obviously timings may vary due to changing conditions and circumstances.

10.00 : Start of lesson. Carry out safety routine.

10.04 : Instructor will review the previous lesson and outline what you will be doing and achieving this lesson.

10.06 : A short drive to enable you to refamiliarise yourself with the car.

10.12 : With the car parked your instructor will give you the necessary briefing for the topic, followed by questions to help you understand the topic. Instructor will demonstrate the manoeuvre if necessary.

10.20 : Practice subject just taught (instructor will 'talk you through' if necessary and correct you either 'on the move' or pull you up to discuss a more serious fault). You will demonstrate that you can carry out the particular aspect being taught.

10.50 : Pull-up to discuss progress so far - any further questions.

10.53 : Drive to original starting point. Instructor will evaluate your progress and inform you of the next lesson's content and relevant reading for you to do to prepare yourself for it . . .

10.58 : Instructor will test your knowledge of highway code questions/signs.

11.00 : End of lesson. Instructor will sign or initial your appointment card to show that the lesson has been given.

To summarise:

* At the start of the lesson you should know which driving tasks you will be covering.

* As the lesson progresses you will be corrected as necessary, either 'on the move' or parked at the side of the road.

* At the end of the lesson you should be informed of your progress and improvement, and what the next lesson will consist of. You will be advised as to what to read to prepare yourself for it.

1.5 Saving time (and money) . . .

On the very first lesson your instructor will check that your eyesight is to the required standard, and that you have a correct valid signed driving licence. If you have not previously paid for the lesson you will generally pay at the start of the lesson. It will save your time (and money) if you have the fee ready - if paying by cheque have it already written out and the cheque card ready to hand to your instructor.

Generally instructors will have 'terms of business', and on your first lesson these will be explained to you. You may have to sign a form to the effect that you have read and understand them. When cancelling a lesson, if less than a specified period of notice (usually 48 hours) is given, you will forfeit the fee.

1.6 Quiet wide roads . . .

Initially your instructor will drive you to a suitable area to start your driving. If possible this will be on quiet wide roads with a minimum of traffic or parked cars. Obviously in certain areas this may be very difficult but your instructor will choose the best available area.

When you arrive at the designated area you will swap seats and your instructor will tell you what the lesson will consist of. At the end of the lesson sufficient time will be allowed to drive you back home.

1.7 Practice with family and friends . . .

Very often pupils will ask . . . "Is it a good thing to practice with friends or relatives?"

Before doing this there are a few points to bear in mind . . .

The car you use to practice in will not have dual controls, therefore it is vital that you can safely control the car; you should be able to correctly steer and position the car so that you and other road users are safe: safety must always be your first consideration.

Although friends and relatives will be very well meaning they will not have had the training or experience that an A.D.I. (Approved Driving Instructor) will have. For this reason it is advisable to only practice what your instructor has taught you, and accept his teaching as being correct and safe; after all he's teaching it all day long and has passed rigorous exams to qualify!

The errors you make as a learner driver will have been, and will continue to be, made many times by other learner drivers. Instructors are able to recognise, assess and rectify such faults. Friends and relatives may not recognise errors or may wrongly identify them. Uncorrected errors not rectified at an early stage will cause problems by recurring at later stages; the longer a fault is left uncorrected or not identified the more difficult it will be to correct later on.

10

1.8 "But my dad says..."

Sometimes the advice and help you receive from friends or relatives will seem to conflict with what your instructor has told you. This is because since they have passed their driving test, friends or relatives will have forgotten, or perhaps have not been taught, the safe and correct procedures for varying traffic situations. Also, being realistic, it is unlikely that they will be driving 'by the book' and may even have developed 'individual' driving styles! Because of this it is unlikely that they will be able to explain precisely and logically a given driving task. Also just because someone may be a 'good' driver it does not necessarily follow that they will be a good teacher!

1.9 Headphones on, brain off...

As a learner driver you will probably have an interest in the way that experienced drivers control their cars. By all means watch and make mental notes but do not criticise other's driving. It is very easy to criticise or to say "That's wrong, you should be doing this..." Most people assume that they are 'good' drivers and do not take kindly to criticism from anybody, least of all learners, so be diplomatic! However, if you see someone driving along with one hand on the gear lever, an elbow on the door frame and headphones on you can draw your own conclusions and stay well clear!

Also you can be sure that the car your instructor uses will be reasonably new, properly insured and mechani- cally sound. It will also be fitted with dual controls and additional interior mirrors so that your instructor can check on following traffic and also check that you are using the interior mirror correctly.

Your instructor will also have any necessary teaching and visuals aids - diagrams, books, videos, etc., on the car.

1.10 How many lessons...?

One question that is asked very frequently by pupils is:
"How many lessons will I need?"

The answer to this depends primarily on the following factors:

* How quickly you learn

* How much practice you get

* How much preparation you do

Age is an important factor when learning to drive. It is generally true that the younger you are the more quickly you will learn a new skill, including driving. A very rough guide is that it will take you 1-1.5 hours for each year of your life; so if you're 17 it could take 17-25 hours.

Your instructor, with experience of teaching people of all ages, will be the best person to advise you on this. Do not ever think that someone is 'too old' - age is no barrier! It will take longer but perseverance will mean eventual success.

1.11 "Six lessons and passed first time . . ."

Everybody learns at their own pace so don't feel pressured into thinking you should be ready for your test after a specific period of time or number of lessons.

You may hear of people who " . . . only had 6 lessons and passed first time . . ." However, they may have forgotten to mention the fact that they have been out practising every evening for 6 months, or didn't reveal the fact that they had already taken one test but " . . . it doesn't count really because I wasn't ready for it . . ."

There are numerous stories and myths about the test - don't believe all you hear - check with your driving instructor; he will have heard most of the stories and can let you know what is fact and what is fiction!

1.12 Follow the road ahead . . .

On your lessons your instructor should use set phrases to instruct and direct you. The directions should be given in the way that they will be phrased on test - this ensures that you become familiar with the terminology used. The phrases are designed to be clear and precise with no room for misunderstanding which could be dangerous.

You should familiarise yourself with the following directional phrases:

Pull up on the left.

Pull up by (named object).

Drive on when you're ready.

At the end of the road turn left (right).

Take the next road on the left (right).

At roundabout, take the road off to the right which is the 3rd exit. (The road layout will dictate the exact phrasing).

Follow the road ahead.

Take the 2nd road on the left.

Take the next available road on the left.

1.13 Time of day/month/year . . .

When you take driving lessons you will sometimes feel you have done very well and at other times feel like giving up! Do not worry about this - we all have good days and bad days and there are various factors to take into consideration:

* Physical and mental well-being

* Worries at home/work

* Attitude/frame of mind

So, when planning your lessons try and ensure that you select times when you will not be too tired or too rushed. If possible allow yourself time to relax before lessons and give some thought to what you have done on previous lessons and what you will be doing on the forthcoming one.

If you just rush into a lesson without adequate preparation you will find that you spend the whole lesson 'catching up with yourself'.

1.14 Sensible driving shoes ...

To get the most out of your driving lessons the following points may be helpful:

* Before your lesson read the pages of this book relevant to the driving tasks that you will be covering.

* Try to relax and think about what you will be doing. Imagine you are sitting in the car and go through the various actions in your mind.

* Prepare any notes or questions you may have.

* Ensure you have the correct money ready, or your cheque written out with cheque card handy.

* Make sure you have the correct footwear (flat or low heeled thin-soled shoes), either wear them or have them with you to change into in the car.

* Also wear clothing that will not get in the way of operating any controls. Avoid wide loose sleeves which could catch on indicator stalks or the gear lever. If you have long hair make sure it is kept off your face. When driving you need to keep both hands on the steering wheel - not brushing hair out of your eyes.

* Immediately after the lesson, whilst it is still fresh in your mind, go over it and think about ways in which your driving could be improved. Read the pages in this book which cover the driving tasks that you spent your lesson practising.

1.15 Driving licence and eyesight check.

Before you start to drive you must have a provisional driving licence which is valid for the vehicle group that you are learning on (cars are Group B - previously Group A - check with your instructor if you're not sure).

The licence must be signed in ink on the front and must be valid. Your driving licence is a valuable document - ensure you keep it safe - it contains information about you - your age and gender as well as name and address.

Your eyesight must be such that you can read a number plate in good daylight at 67ft./20.5m. (about 5 car lengths). If you need to wear glasses or contact lenses to do this then you must wear them to drive.

Bear in mind that this is a minimum legal requirement and is only 50% of perfect vision. If you find you have difficulty in distinguishing between certain letters, i.e. D, O, G, C, etc., it would be advisable to visit your optician. Also bear in mind that poor vision will become even worse at night or in twilight conditions.

Being colour blind, or even having only one eye, is no bar to driving as long as you can satisfy the minimum legal eyesight requirement.

Remember though, that no matter how perfect your eyesight, it won't do you any good unless you learn to look properly. More about that later . . .

1.16 The Driving Test

Your instructor will initially be 'talking you through' various driving tasks but ultimately you will be making decisions and thinking for yourself, with the instructor giving you DIRECTIONS only, rather than INSTRUCTION.

Your will be ready to take your test when you can drive consistently well, confidently and safely WITHOUT assistance and guidance from your instructor.

The driving test is covered in detail, with all aspects explained clearly and precisely, in the book "The Driving Test : Graphic Traffic Version" which was written by the author of this book. It is available from all good bookstores. If you have any difficulty locating the above book please contact the publisher.

QUESTIONS THAT LEARNER DRIVERS ASK . . .

1.17 How soon before I start learning should I book lessons?

About six weeks before. Most instructors generally work well in advance; so the more notice you can give the better. This especially applies if you want to take lessons at the more popular times, i.e. evening/weekends.

1.18 How much should I pay for lessons?

There is no 'set' price for tuition and the cost will vary considerably (£7 - £17 per lesson) depending on the following factors: area of the U.K. that you live in, length of lesson, time of day, national driving school or independent operator. The larger driving schools will charge more because of their offices (rents, rates, advertising, staff wages, etc.), but it does not follow that the larger the school the better the instructor! The vast majority of instructors are self-employed and standards will vary.

Be aware that for evening and weekends lessons, some instructors will charge more.

The fee for taking a test in a driving school car will usually be three times the lesson price.

1.19 What should I ask the instructor when I book lessons?

Firstly, make sure that he covers your area, and the times that he gives instruction, i.e. Monday to Saturday, 9.30 a.m. to 7.00 p.m. inc. You should then go on to ask if lessons are structured, and whether progress reports will be given.

Any instructor giving tuition for payment must be a Department of Transport Approved Driving Instructor

(A.D.I.) and display a valid green certificate of registration or be a Licensed Trainee Instructor and display a red licence; (whichever is displayed must show the name, and a photograph, of the instructor).

The certificate or licence, must be displayed in the windscreen whilst tuition is being given.

You should ask him what other qualifications he holds; these might include the following:

* Advanced Driver (Member of the Institute of Advanced Motorists or R.o.S.P.A. Advanced Drivers Association).

* Holder of a Diploma in Driving Instruction.

* Cardington 'Special' Driving Test Grade 'A'.

* DIAmond Advanced Instructor.

* A specific teaching qualification:
  City & Guilds 730.
  B.Sc./B.A.
  NJC Tutor.

Any instructor who takes a keen interest in his work will not mind being asked any of the above. If you get vague or evasive answers, go elsewhere!

Also, you may wish to have a non-smoking instructor so ask about this.

Check if there will be other pupils in the car, and verify where you want to be collected from - most instructors operate a free collection service.

You may also want to know what sort of car he uses - how new it is, etc.

Pass rate. The national pass rate is 52%. Ask your instructor what HIS first time pass rate is. An instructor taking a keen interest in his work will be keeping a record of passes and will be able to tell you what percentage of his pupils pass first time.

1.20 When I book lessons what information will the instructor want from me?

Initially, the area that you live in, then your name, address and phone number.

He may also ask for your driver number (on your driving licence) so have that to hand.

He will want to know what times you are available. Be prepared to be flexible and consider lunchtimes, days off, starting work later/finishing earlier, holidays, etc.

He may also tell you the fee structure, terms of business and how to pay (i.e. in advance, cheques up to £50 with bankers card, etc.) He may ask you about previous driving experience. Try to be as precise as possible with this information - it will help the instructor to get an idea of what standard you will be at.

He will ask if you wear glasses or contact lenses and, if so, he will want you to bring them along for your lessons.

1.21 Previous experience . . .

If you have been, or still are, a cyclist, moped rider or motorcyclist, this will have given you a good grounding in 'road sense' and you will be used to being on the road amongst traffic.

Also, if you play racquet sports (squash, tennis, etc.) this can improve your eye-to-hand co-ordination, something which plays an important part in making judgements when driving.

Keyboard playing can help - again the eye-to-hand co-ordination (with foot pedals on some pianos) will help a learner to carry out different tasks at the same time.

However, if none of the above applies to you, do not worry; and, if you are a cycling piano-playing squash player, do not automatically expect that you will be an expert driver! It may just help though . . .

1.22 Advice from your Instructor

If your A.D.I. has advised you to postpone a driving test he will explain to you the reason why, and you should listen carefully to this advice - it is for your own (and others) safety. This particularly applies to parents who sometimes think that just because they have spent X amount on lessons over Y months that you should take the test! Or perhaps feel that their son, or daughter should take the test "for the experience"!! If your instructor had advised you to postpone the test and you insist on taking it, it will be the examiner who has the experience, and not a pleasant one at that.

So parents - remember that driving is a life skill and acquisition of the necessary skills has no direct link to the amount of time or money spent on lessons - accept the advice of an A.D.I. After all they have the training, experience and knowledge to accurately assess a pupil's level of driving skills.

1.23 SUMMARY: Driving lessons

* Get yourself in the right frame of mind.

* Think about what you will be doing on the lesson.

* Prepare thoroughly for the lesson.

* Make sure you wear comfortable clothes and correct footwear.

* Listen carefully to the advice given by your professional driving instructor (A.D.I.) - it is in your own interest.

NOTE: If you need to wear glasses to drive be aware that thick frames and side pieces may obstruct your vision to the sides. Consider thinner frames or contact lenses for optimum vision. Carry a spare pair in the car with you.

2

IN THE DRIVING SEAT / MOVING OFF (UP-HILL, DOWNHILL AND ANGLED STARTS)

2.1 Getting into the car

On your first lesson your instructor will drive you to a reasonably quiet area where he will explain the controls of the car: what they are and what they do. You will swap seats, putting you in the driving seat.

Before you open the car door, getting in or out, always check around to ensure that you will not inconvenience or endanger other road users, especially cyclists or pedestrians. Get into the car briskly and close the door firmly without slamming it.

2.2 The safety routine

Each time you get in a car as a driver there is a safety routine or cockpit drill to be carried out: this routine is known as D.S.S.S.M.

Each letter stands for a word, as follows:

D : DOORS: It is the driver's responsibility to make sure that all doors are shut securely. Do not lock (in an emergency, you may need to be freed and a locked door would cause unnecessary delay).

Using the door handle pull the door

firmly closed, check that it does not rattle (if it does it means it is not closed properly).

Check your passengers' doors are closed properly: ask them to check!

S : SEAT: Adjust your seat to a practical driving position. This will mean that you can push the clutch pedal right down with your left foot with a slight bend at the knee, with your thigh pressed firmly onto the seat. Your leg should not be stretched, or be knocking against the dashboard.

Most seats can be adjusted in various ways (forward, backwards, up or down, plus back of seat) - make sure it is adjusted to the most practical position for you.

HEAD RESTRAINTS: Head restraints are fitted in order to greatly reduce the risk of 'whiplash' injury to the neck. 'Whiplash' happens when one vehicle runs into the back of another. The impact of the collision will cause the occupants' heads to snap back suddenly; if no head restraints are fitted the result could be severe neck injury. This could mean having to wear a neck brace, time off work, severe inconvenience, etc. A properly adjusted head restraint will prevent this.

Head restraints are NOT designed to be used as a rest for your head, when driving. Do not be tempted to remove the head restraint in order to improve viiability when reversing; it is up to you to look around it. Adjust the head restraint so that the point of contact would be at the rearmost point of your skull.

S : STEERING WHEEL: Place both hands on the wheel at 12 o'clock (as on a clock face) and run them round to 6 and back to 12. This is to check that you have freedom of movement with no obstructions, i.e. clothing, jewellery, build. In winter extra clothes may hinder so remove outer garments: overcoats, etc.

S : SEAT-BELT: Fix buckle into anchor point. Make sure it is secured. Remove any twists or kinks. W h e n releasing the belt, hold buckle and feed back. Check that belt will lock - give it a sharp tug with your right hand - after all, you wouldn't want to find it wasn't working when you go through the windscreen!

It is the responsibility of each individual over 14 years of age to ensure that a seat-belt is worn. It is the driver's responsibility to ensure that children under 14 are 'suitably restrained'.

It is a legal requirement to wear your seat-belt. Your chances of surviving a road accident increase by 50% when wearing a seat-belt.

REAR SEAT-BELTS
Rear seat-belts have been compulsorily fitted to all new cars from April 1987. If fitted, it is now a legal requirement to wear them. Obviously, in the event of an accident, unrestrained passengers will be thrown forward causing further injury (possibly fatal) to the front seat occupants.

The law which came into force on 1st September 1989 gives greater protection to children in the back seats of cars. Children under 14 years must be restrained in rear seats wherever appropriate restraints are available. In practice, this means the restraint must be correct for the child's weight. (Any purpose-made child restraint must by law carry a label showing its 'design weight'.) An appropriate restraint' includes an adult belt used in conjunction with a booster cushion for children aged 1-3 years, or on its own for children aged 4 years and over. If an appropriate restraint is available when a child is in the car, the child must use it. However, you can still carry children in cars which lack rear seat-belts, (or take more children than there are restraints available). Though perhaps you should think of installing rear seat-belts or child restraints anyway, for safety's sake.

Please note : It is now a legal requirement that back seat passengers must wear seat-belts (if they are fitted).

SEAT-BELT EXEMPTIONS

You need not wear a seat-belt If:-

1. You have a valid medical exemption certificate.

2. Your vehicle is not required to have belts fitted because of its age or type. If your vehicle was first registered after 31 December 1964 you must wear seat-belts. If it is older than that it will be exempt. However, if seat-belts have since been fitted they must be worn.

3. You are driving a vehicle and carrying out a manoeuvre which includes reversing, or are a qualified driver (full British licence holder) supervising a learner driver (provisional licence h o l d e r) carrying out such a manoeuvre.

4. You are driving a taxi displaying a plate showing the vehicle is licensed as such, when plying for hire or carrying passengers.

5. You are driving a private hire vehicle when carrying a passenger for hire. The vehicle must carry a plate showing that it is licensed as a private hire vehicle or at the hackney carriage rate.

6. You are engaged on local collection and delivery work and are driving a vehicle which is constructed or adapted for that purpose.

7. The seat-belt becomes defective on a journey, or if you have made arrangements for repairs or replacement of the belt, i.e. you are driving to the garage or repair shop.

8. The inertia type belt becomes locked by virtue of the position of the vehicle on an incline. The belt must be worn as soon as the mechanism becomes unlocked.

9. You are driving a vehicle on trade plates and are examining or repairing a mechanical fault.

10. You are occupying the centre front seat and there are two other persons occupying the other front seats. With only the driver and one front seat passenger, the passenger must wear a seat-belt irrespective of which front seat is occupied.

The financial penalty for not wearing a seat-belt (unless exempt) is £50. The more serious penalty is the fact that not wearing a seat-belt will more than double the risk of being killed or seriously injured in an accident.

M : MIRRORS: Most cars will have 3 rear view mirrors: 1 interior and 2 exterior (either door or wing mounted). It is vital that the mirrors are adjusted properly so that you can make effective use of them and be aware of what is happening behind and to the side of your vehicle.

The interior mirror will give you a life-size image of following traffic, whereas the exterior mirrors are usually convex (slightly curved) which makes the reflected image look smaller and further away. You will notice this when sitting in the driver's seat and looking from the interior mirror to the exterior mirrors.

To adjust the interior mirror place your left thumb on the lower left-hand corner of the mirror and your left forefinger on the top left-hand corner. Do not touch the glass when doing this. Do the same thing with the forefinger on the right-hand side of the mirror. You will now be able to adjust the mirror - it is on a swivel joint and should move easily allowing you to position it correctly

Line up the top of the mirror with the top of the back window. In the right hand side of the mirror you should see the edge of your left ear, or hair (left side).

Adjust the door mirrors so that in the lower left hand corner of the drivers door mirror you can see the door security button (if fitted), and the base of the door pillar. Ideally the lower edge of   the door mirror should be parallel to the ground.

Adjust the passenger door mirror so that in the lower right hand corner of the mirror you can see the door security button (if fitted) and the base of the door pillar. The lower edge of this mirror should also be parallel to the ground.

Door mirrors are adjusted either manually from inside (or outside of the car) or electrically from inside, make sure you can adjust both mirrors without help, and always make all adjustments before moving away.

These safety checks are done in a logical order:

Doors / Seat / Steering Wheel / Seat-Belt /Mirrors.

Obviously it is more logical to adjust the mirrors last, after having adjusted your seat to a practical driving position.

SAFETY ROUTINE

1. Doors

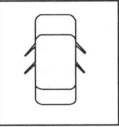

All closed properly ?

1. **DOORS**
2. **SEAT**
3. **STEERING WHEEL**
4. **SEAT BELTS**
5. **MIRRORS**

2. Seat

Adjusted Properly ?

4. Seat - Belts

Is your belt properly fixed ?

3. Steering Wheel

Free movement of hands around the wheel ?

5. Mirrors

All adjusted properly ?

2.3 The controls of the vehicle

For the purposes of instruction it is assumed that the vehicle is conventional: manually operated, right-hand drive.

There are three types of control in the vehicle:

* Hand controls
* Foot controls
* Visual controls.

HAND CONTROLS

Starting with the hand controls, the first one is the handbrake or parking brake, usually located between the two front seats. This brake is only to be used when the vehicle is stationary and is used to secure the vehicle. The handbrake or parking brake operates only on the *rear wheels. If it were to be used when the vehicle was moving, the rear wheels could lock (stop turning) and the vehicle could skid. Always bring the vehicle to a COMPLETE stop with the footbrake, and then apply the handbrake.

Generally, when the vehicle is stationary for more than a moment (at junctions, in stop-start traffic, etc.) the handbrake should be applied.

A moment is defined here as the time it takes to apply and release the handbrake without causing unnecessary delay.

TO APPLY THE HANDBRAKE: Grip it with your left hand and with your left thumb push and hold in the button at the end of the handbrake; this will release the catch or ratchet allowing you to pull up the handbrake smoothly and silently (if you hear the ratchet noise each time you use the handbrake this will eventually wear and could cause the handbrake to release itself allowing the car to roll downhill causing extreme danger).

When you have pulled up the handbrake firmly as far as it will go, release your left thumb from the button - this will enable the handbrake to 'lock' into position.

TO RELEASE THE HANDBRAKE: Grip it with you left hand and pull the handbrake up slightly further; this will enable you to push in the button with your left thumb. Keeping the button pushed in, lower the handbrake fully to the floor and then replace your left hand on the steering wheel.

Instructions will be given as follows:
Apply the handbrake
Release the handbrake

* On some foreign cars the handbrake operates on the front wheels : check your handbook.

GEAR LEVER

This is usually floor-mounted and is used to change from one gear to another. Only to be used by the left hand.

The gears enable the driver to match the engine power to the speed of the vehicle and its load (passengers, luggage, etc.) This is done by changing to a different gear which brings a different size of gear wheel into contact with the drive from the engine.

The gear lever will generally have 6 positions.

There will usually be a diagram on the top of the gear lever indicating these positions.

4 forward gears (some vehicles have a 5th forward gear)
1 reverse - Do not put vehicle into reverse whilst vehicle is moving
1 neutral (not in any gear)

The gears are used consecutively as the speed of the vehicle increases:

SPEEDS IN GEARS (LEVEL ROAD)

1st	0-5 mph
2nd	5-15 mph
3rd	15-25 mph
4th	25+ mph

Obviously these speeds will vary depending on gradient of road and size of engine. Check with your handbook, or instructor.

1st gear has a lot of power but not much speed, and then as you go through the gears you get more speed and less power. 4th has the widest speed range: from 25 mph (level road) up to the car's maximum speed (conditions permitting!).

2nd and 3rd gears are working gears - do most of the work, especially in traffic.

4th gear is a cruising or economical gear. A fifth gear, if fitted, is usually an 'overdrive'; very useful for economical motorway driving.

As a guideline, on a level road it should take you approximately 10 seconds to go from rest to 30 mph changing consecutively through the gears.

To select the gear you need, first push the clutch pedal right down. Then you can move the gear lever into the correct position for the gear you want. Whenever you change from one gear to another the gear lever always moves through neutral.

NEUTRAL POSITION: When the gear lever is in neutral, the link between the engine and driven wheels is broken. The driven wheels may be the two front (front wheel drive, FWD), the two rear (rear wheel drive, RWD) or all four wheels (4WD).

Each time before you start the engine, you must check that it is in neutral. Compare the feel of the gear lever in neutral; there will be much more free movement from side to side as compared with 1st or 2nd gear.

Also, the position of the gear lever will give you an indication as to whether it is in neutral or not.

The gear lever does not need to be forced into position. If the correct grip is used all that is needed is a firm positive movement.

To select 1st gear put your hand on the gear lever, with your palm away from you. Push forward firmly into 1st gear.

To select 2nd gear from 1st gear, place your left hand on the gear lever palm away from you and move the gear lever down with a firm and positive movement.

To select 3rd gear from 2nd gear, place your left hand on the gear lever palm towards you and move the gear lever firmly and positively into neutral, over towards you and then forward into 3rd gear.

To select 4th gear from 3rd gear, place your left hand on the gear lever palm towards you and move the lever down positively and firmly.

When building up speed always change through the gears consecutively, i.e. 1-2-3-4 without missing any gears out.

However, when selecting a lower gear it is safer and quite acceptable to change down from 4th to 2nd gear missing out 3rd gear, or even 4th to 1st (when coming to a give-way line where your view is restricted, for example).

This is called SELECTIVE gear changing and, as well as being logical and safe, it is kinder to the vehicle; creating less wear and tear on the mechanics of the vehicle.

Any necessary reduction in speed to change down from one gear to a lower one is made by use of the footbrake.

CORRECT POSITION FOR HANDS ON THE STEERING WHEEL

Correct '10 to 2'
(as on a clock face)

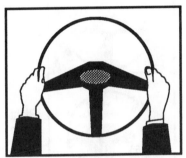

Correct '¼ to 3'
(as on a clock face)

Use whichever of the above feels most comfortable.

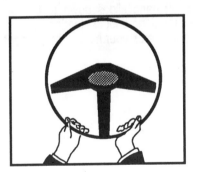

Incorrect (Too low)

Incorrect (Too high)

THE PULL-PUSH METHOD OF STEERING

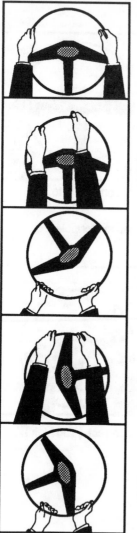

This example illustrates how to steer to the right.

'Normal' position of hands on the wheel.

Right hand slides up to 12 o'clock ready to 'pull' down. Pulling down from 12 will give the maximum leverage on the steering wheel, left hand stays as is.

Right hand grips the wheel and PULLS DOWN to 6, while left hand slides down to 6. On manoeuvres requiring a lot of steering (turn-in-the-road, parking etc), your hands should meet at 6.

Left hand now grips the wheel and PUSHES UP to 12, while right hand slides up to 12 to meet it.

Right hand grips wheel and pulls down to 6, while left hand slides down to meet it.

REMEMBER: GEARS FOR GO, BRAKES FOR SLOW!

To select a lower gear, i.e. from 4th to 2nd, place your hand on the gear lever palm away from you. Move the lever into neutral and away from you and down into 2nd gear.

The reverse gear must **only** be selected when the vehicle is stationary. If your vehicle is fitted with reversing lights, one or two white lights will show at the back of the vehicle to warn other road users of your intention when the reverse gear is engaged.

The position of the reverse gear will depend on the make of your car - look for a diagram on top of the gear lever, or ask your instructor.

When selecting gears, you must keep your eyes on the road, not looking at the gear lever.

Instructions will be given as follows:
Select (named) gear
Select the most appropriate for the speed of the car.

STEERING WHEEL

The next hand control is the steering wheel which is located on top of the steering column and is used to change the direction of the vehicle. The steering wheel moves the two front wheels only (there is one production vehicle with four wheel steering, but this is very rare).

The steering wheel should be held lightly but firmly, as though you are holding eggs, with your hands at ten-to-two or quarter-to-three (as on a clock face), whichever feels more comfortable for you. Both hands must be kept on the wheel at all times, apart from when you are changing gear, giving arm signals or operating any minor control.

Do not cross your hands when steering, use the pull-push method as illustrated.

As a turn is completed, the vehicle must be straightened up and to do this the steering wheel must be fed back through your hands, not allowed to spin back on its own - this greatly reduces the amount of control you have over the vehicle.

When steering look where you want to go. Do not look at the kerb, central white line or parked cars but look as far ahead as you can, also scanning the road from side to side with your eyes.
If, when driving, you find yourself veering to one side or the other it usually means that you are not looking far enough ahead.
Do not grip the wheel tightly; to maintain a steady course you will need minor adjustments to the left or right; generally movements of 1 to 2 inches/ 2.5 cm to 5 cm will be sufficient to keep the car on a straight course. Do not turn the wheel excessively when driving on a straight course. The higher the speed the more minimal but precise any steering movements will need to be. Do not snatch or jerk the wheel suddenly as

this will alarm and confuse other road users and cause the car to veer and swerve unnecessarily and dangerously.

Do not turn the steering wheel when the car is stationary; this causes excessive strain on the steering mechanism and linkage leading to premature wear and possible danger from component failure.

POWER ASSISTED STEERING (PAS): Some vehicles are fitted with this as an aid to steering at low speeds and it takes a lot less effort to turn the wheel. Because of this the temptation is greater to turn the wheel when the car is stationary but try and avoid this; it puts a great deal of strain on the steering mechanism and power steering unit. It also wears the tyres. Be aware that when changing from a car without power steering to one with you will find that you are over-steering (steering too much) because the same amount of effort produces a greater steering effect when it is power assisted.

DIRECTION INDICATORS

A stalk at the side of the steering column will control the direction indicators which are fitted at the front and rear (sometimes at sides) of vehicles to indicate your intentions to other road users. They can be orange or may be white on older vehicles and will flash at between 60 to 120 times per minute.

Always remember to cancel a signal once you have completed a manoeuvre. If you do not do this it could mislead others with possible dangerous results.

LIGHTING

AT FRONT OF VEHICLE:
TWO WHITE PARKING LIGHTS (USUALLY CONTAINED WITHIN THE HEADLIGHT) USE WHEN THE VEHICLE IS STATIONARY, ENGINE OFF.

TWO WHITE DIM/DIP LIGHTS (USUALLY CONTAINED WITHIN THE HEADLIGHT) 1/6 AS BRIGHT AS DIPPED, TO BE USED IN WELL LIT BUILT-UP AREA.

TWO WHITE DIPPED HEAD-LIGHTS, USE WHEN MAIN BEAMS WOULD DAZZLE

TWO WHITE MAIN BEAM HEAD-LIGHTS, USE ONLY WHERE THEY WOULD NOT DAZZLE OTHER ROAD USERS.

AT THE REAR OF VEHICLE:
TWO RED REAR LIGHTS

WHITE NUMBER PLATE ILLUMINATION

ONE OR TWO FOG LIGHTS (HIGH INTENSITY RED LIGHTS), USED ONLY IN CONDITIONS OF REDUCED VISIBILITY, I.E. LESS THAN 100m.

DO NOT USE THEM JUST BECAUSE IT IS DARK/RAINING/MISTY.

HAZARD WARNING LIGHTS

When the hazard warning light switch is on, both front and both rear indicators will flash at the same time and show that you are causing a hazard.

Use the hazard warning lights only when you are causing a temporary obstruction due to an accident or emergency. It is illegal to use them when the car is moving, except to warn others briefly if you have to slow down quickly on a motorway or unrestricted (70 mph) dual carriageway.

The position of the various hand controls will vary from car to car. Make sure you familiarise yourself with them.

The hand controls include:
   Windscreen wipers/washers
   Ventilation/heating system
   Choke control
   Rear wiper/washer
   Heated rear window

THE HORN

Usually located either at the end of the indicator stalk or in the centre of the steering wheel.

The horn is to be used only to make others aware of your presence - do not use it angrily or as a rebuke. Do not use the horn in a built-up area between 11.30 p.m. and 7.00 a.m.

HEADLAMP FLASH

Usually operated by pulling the light control stalk towards you, the headlamp flash has the same meaning as the horn: to let others know you are there.

DO NOT USE IT FOR ANYTHING ELSE AS THE MEANING COULD BE MISINTERPRETED, PUTTING YOURSELF OR OTHERS IN DANGER.

FOOT CONTROLS

Looking at the pedals from right to left they are:
accelerator, brake, clutch.

THE ACCELERATOR

Starting with the accelerator, when this pedal is pushed down it injects more petrol into the engine, giving more power and therefore more speed. For the purposes of instruction, the accelerator will be referred to as the gas pedal - it is easier and quicker to say.

The gas pedal should be used smoothly and gently, never harshly, and only with your right foot.

The instructions given for the gas pedal will be: less gas, more gas, off the gas and set the gas.

Set the gas means press the pedal down a certain amount and hold it there keeping your right foot absolutely still (or set).

When driving along, the vehicle can be slowed down by taking your foot off the gas; this is deceleration.

THE FOOTBRAKE

The middle pedal is the footbrake. This pedal operates the brakes on all four wheels, and is the most efficient method of slowing the car down.

The brake pedal is to be used only by the right foot.

The brake pedal must be used **PROGRESSIVELY.** This means starting off pushing the pedal lightly and then increasing the pressure to bring the vehicle to a stop. Just before the vehicle comes to rest, relax the pressure (raise your right foot slightly) on the brake pedal; this will avoid a sudden jolt when the vehicle stops.

The instructions given for the brake will be:

> **cover the brake (foot over brake but not pressing down)**
> **gently brake**
> **gently brake to a stop.**

To operate the accelerator and brake correctly and safely your right heel should be firmly placed on the floor at a point between the brake and the accelerator. Keeping your heel on the floor your right foot can now pivot from gas to brake quickly and smoothly as necessary.

THE CLUTCH

The next pedal is the clutch. This is used only by the left foot and this is used to disconnect the engine from the driven wheels to enable you to select 1st and reverse gear, change from one gear to another or into neutral.

Basically the clutch mechanism consists of two plates which when joined (clutch pedal up) enable the power to be transmitted from the engine to the wheels and therefore allow the vehicle to be driven.
It is called the clutch because one plate 'clutches' at the other to join the plates together.

When the plates are apart (clutch pedal down) the link is broken and the engine is disconnected, and the vehicle will 'coast' (free-wheel), going along under its own momentum. Because one of the plates is revolving and the other is not, the clutch pedal must be brought up **SLOWLY** to enable these plates to join together smoothly. If the clutch is not brought up smoothly and slowly the vehicle will jump or 'kangaroo'.

Each time the clutch comes up think of the two plates coming together: **SMOOTHLY!**

The instructions given for the clutch will be:

Cover the clutch (foot over clutch but do not press down);

Clutch down (clutch can go down as quickly as you can push it down);

Clutch up smoothly (bring clutch up slowly and smoothly);

Rest your left foot (when not using the clutch the left foot should be resting flat on the floor, NOT under or over the clutch);

Find the biting point (a change in the engine note will indicate when the clutch plates are just touching. At this point keep your left foot absolutely still and then when ready to move away a slight upward movement of the clutch will bring the clutch plates together, causing the vehicle to move).

Note: The clutch will need to be pushed down completely:

1. When selecting gears, and

2. Just before the vehicle stops to prevent the engine from stalling.

To operate the clutch correctly and safely your left heel should be placed firmly on the floor directly in front of the clutch pedal and then place the ball of your left foot on the clutch pedal and push down.

VISUAL CONTROLS

Always keep your windscreen and windows clean and clear.

Make sure you know where the blind spots are on the vehicle you are driving. A blind spot is an area not covered by your interior and exterior mirrors. Also anything that you cannot see through is a blind spot.

The following are common blind spots:

1. Windscreen pillars.
2. Door pillars.
3. Hatchback pillars.
4. Head restraints.
5. Passengers (front and rear).
6. Rear spoilers.

It is up to YOU as driver to move your head to look around these blind spots; always assume that another road user is hidden in a blind spot.

The visual controls in the instrument panel will usually consist of:

PETROL GAUGE: This tells you how much petrol is in the petrol tank of your vehicle. The gauge will be marked in litres or gallons. Be aware that different vehicles hold different amounts of petrol - a mini will hold 5.5 gallons / 30 litres while a Rolls Royce may hold 25 gallons / 150 litres. Also familiarise yourself with your vehicle's expected fuel consumption; from this you can work out approximately how much further you can travel before you will need to fill up again.

Never let the petrol gauge get too low because sediment in the bottom of the tank could get sucked through, causing damage to the more delicate parts of the engine such as the fuel pump or carburettor.

WATER TEMPERATURE GAUGE: This measures the temperature of the water that cools the engine. Water circulates around the engine through a series of holes and passageways.

This water absorbs heat from the engine, keeping it cool. The hot water is then circulated through the radiator at the front of the car which cools it due to air flow. This cooled water then recirculates around the engine and the cycle carries on like so.

If the temperature gauge registers H (hot) stop at a convenient place and seek advice. There are many reasons why a vehicle might overheat - generally the most common factor is lack of water in the system.

Normal running is halfway on the gauge - keep a regular check.

SPEEDOMETER: This measures the speed of the vehicle. There will generally be a milometer as well, which records the total mileage covered by the vehicle and a trip meter which can be used to measure journeys and then reset back to zero.

Dependent on the make of vehicle any other visual controls will be explained to you by your instructor.

2.4 Starting the engine

It is assumed here that the ignition is on the right-hand side of the steering column. The engine is started with the ignition key - a removable key that on most modern cars also unlocks the doors and boot.

Before starting the engine there are two checks to make:

1. Make sure that the handbrake is applied.

2. Make sure that the gear lever is in neutral.

If the vehicle is started with the gear lever in a position other than neutral it would jump forwards (or backwards if the gear lever is in reverse).

Hold the steering wheel with your left hand. This is to give you control of the steering should the vehicle be started accidentally in gear. On older vehicles a worn and loose gearbox may lead you to think that neutral has been selected when in fact the gear lever may be in first gear.

Insert the key into the ignition and with your right hand turn the key away from you until it clicks into position - this will free the steering lock (if fitted). Turn the key away from you again until it clicks into position. This position will activate the electrical circuit, so that ancillary items such as radio, wipers, heated rear screen can be used if required, when the car is parked without having to have the engine running.

Turn the key away from you again and it will click into position. At this stage the warning lights on the instrument panel should be illuminated.

The purpose of this is a visual check to make sure that the warning light BULBS are working - after all if the bulb (costing 50p) was not working you might not be warned that your engine was about to seize through lack of oil (cost of engine £500!) So, take note of any warning lights and ensure that any bulbs not working are replaced immediately!

To start the engine turn the key away from you again and hold it there for a second or two and then release it. The engine should now be running. If not, repeat the procedure as above immediately.

When starting a cold engine the choke control may need to be used. Many cars have automatic chokes but if your car has a manual choke control you would need to pull out the control as far as it will go and then start the engine.

The reason a cold engine needs this is that the engine runs on a mixture of petrol and air, and a cold engine needs the amount of petrol to air increased. The choke does this by 'choking' off the air supply, i.e. either partially or almost completely blocking off the air supply so that less air is mixed with the petrol. When the engine has warmed up the choke control can be eased back to the off position.

How long this takes will depend on several factors:
* Outside air temperature
* Condition of the engine
* Operating efficiency of the choke control

2.5 Moving off

Before moving off assess whether you are on a level, uphill or downhill. This may be very obvious in some cases but where there is some doubt look at the base of any brick walls - the line will assist you in deciding whether it is level, downhill or uphill.

The sequence for moving off is as follows:
It is assumed that you are parked by the kerb on the left-hand side of the road.

2.5.1 LEVEL START/FLAT ROAD

1. Clutch down and keep it down.
2. Hand on gear lever, palm away from you.
3. Select first gear.
4. Set the gas (about the thickness of two pound coins).
5. Slowly clutch up until the engine note changes *slightly.*
6. Keep both feet still.
7. Observation routine:
   Check left shoulder blind spot
   Passenger door mirror
   Interior mirror
   Driver's door mirror
   Right shoulder blind spot
   Ahead
   Interior mirror
   (This is in effect almost a 360° sweep left to right)
8. Indicate right if necessary*
9. Release handbrake and replace left hand on steering wheel.
10. Clutch up slightly (thickness of one pound coin); when the car starts to move keep your left foot still.
11. Steer slightly right to move away from kerb.
12. Steer left to a normal driving position (3ft/1m from kerb).
13. Clutch fully and smoothly up, rest your left foot on the floor.
14. Check mirrors, if safe a little more gas.

* A signal will only be necessary if it would help or warn other road users: drivers, cyclists or pedestrians. DO NOT signal automatically, regardless of other road users. It is vital that you look properly, then decide whether a signal is required, before you move away. This means taking in all the surrounding information and analysing it to see how you might affect other road users or vice versa.

2.5.2 MOVING AWAY UPHILL

1. Clutch down and keep it down.
2. Hand on gear lever, palm away from you.
3. Select first gear.
4. Set the gas (more than for a level start; the steeper the hill, the more gas you will need).
5. Find the biting point (listen for the engine note changing).
6. At the biting point keep your left foot still.
7. Observation routine:
   Check left shoulder blind spot
   Passenger door mirror
   Interior mirror
   Driver's door Mirror
   Right shoulder blind spot
   Ahead
   Interior mirror
   (This is in effect almost a 360° sweep from left to right)
   Although this may seem to involve a great deal it really involves turning your head to yhr right and then to the left.
8. Indicate if necessary.
9. Release handbrake.
10. Increase the gas slightly.
11. Bring the clutch up a small amount.

12. Steer slightly to the right to move away from the kerb.
13. Steer to the left to a normal driving position (3ft/1m from kerb).
14. Clutch smoothly and fully up, rest left foot on floor.
15. Check mirrors, if safe more gas.

As you will notice, the main difference with the uphill start is that you do not release the handbrake until the clutch is at the biting point. Failure to do this would result in the car rolling backwards. If the clutch was up too far the car could stall. Finding the correct balance on the clutch takes practice - also make sure you are wearing very thin-soled shoes; those will help you to get the 'feel' of the clutch biting point.

2.5.3 A PERFECT HILL START EVERYTIME...

One way to achieve this is to find an uphill gradient (not too steep) and practice 'holding' the car absolutely still without using the handbrake or footbrake.

Hold the car perfectly still for 3 to 4 seconds and drive forward about 2m/6ft, and hold the car still, using only the clutch pedal. Then drive forward another 2m, and so on. This exercise will help you to gain full understanding of clutch control. Your instructor will demonstrate it to you, and then you should practice it.

With practice you should soon be able to move off from rest on an uphill gradient and then stop and hold the car absolutely still, using only the clutch pedal.

Each time you move off, remember

to check properly, especially over your shoulder (blind spot). This applies even if you are only driving forward a very short distance.

2.5.4 MOVING AWAY DOWNHILL

1. Clutch down and keep it down.
2. Hand on gear lever, palm away from you.
3. Select first gear.
4. Right foot on footbrake, press firmly.
5. Release handbrake.
6. Observation routine:
   Check left shoulder blind spot
   Passenger door mirror
   Interior mirror
   Driver's door mirror
   Right shoulder blind spot
   Ahead
   Interior mirror
(This is in effect almost a 360° sweep from left to right)
Although this may seem to involve a great deal it really involves turning your head to the right and then to the left.
7. Indicate if necessary.
8. Gently release footbrake to start vehicle rolling.
9. Clutch up smoothly as footbrake is released.
10. Steer slightly to the right to move away from the kerb.
11. Steer to the left to a normal driving position (3ft/1 m from kerb).
12. Check mirrors, if safe more gas.

Note: On steeper gradients it is possible to move away in 2nd gear.

When you have mastered each of the above starts you will then be ready to be taught the next logical driving task:

2.5.5 THE ANGLED START (moving away from behind a parked vehicle)

This will combine either moving away on a level road, uphill or downhill coordinating the steering so that you allow sufficient clearance to the vehicle you are moving away from. Because the speed of your vehicle needs to be very slow (to give you time to steer) you will need to be especially careful when checking your blind spot (over right shoulder) and will need to do this several times.

2.6 SUMMARY

Each of the various starts needs to be practised until you can correctly assess each start and then demonstrate that you can move away safely:

1. On a level road
2. Uphill
3. Downhill
4. From behind a parked vehicle (angled start)

To do each of these starts competently and safely, you need to:

* Check mirrors and blind spot to take effective rearward observation.

* Co-ordinate the controls properly to give a smooth controlled start.

3

MAKING NORMAL STOPS

3.1 Where?

Having decided that you are going to stop, choose a place that is safe, convenient and legal.

What this means in practice is that you should not:

* Park across or very close to drives

* Park on a bus stop

* Park too close to a junction (Not less than 15m daytime or 10m night-time)

* Opposite or nearly opposite a parked car (obviously in some roads you may not be able to do otherwise).

These are just a few examples. The Highway Code comprehensively lists places where you should not and must not park.

3.2 How? ...

The sequence to use for stopping is:

    Mirror
    Signal (if necessary)
    Manoeuvre

Your actions should be as follows:

1. Check your mirrors, decide whether to give a signal or not.

2. Off the gas.

3. Gently brake, then progressively increase the pressure on the brake pedal.

4. Just before the vehicle stops, push the clutch down to prevent the engine stalling.

5. As the vehicle stops, relax the pressure on the footbrake slightly: this will prevent the vehicle jolting to a stop.

6. When the vehicle has completely stopped, apply the handbrake.

7. Put the gear lever into neutral.

8. Rest your feet.

9. Cancel your indicator if a signal has been given.

It is quite acceptable to stop in the gear you happen to be in. Changing down through the gears is completely unnecessary when you know you are going to stop anyway, for example:

* At a red traffic light.

* When stopping to park.

When stopping at junction with give way markings, select first gear and use the handbrake if the vehicle is going to be stopped for more than a moment. A moment here is defined as the time it takes to apply and release the handbrake without causing unnecessary delay.

At solid white stop lines at traffic lights and stop signs (octagonal stop) bring the vehicle to a complete stop, apply the handbrake and then select first gear.

Solid white stop lines are used where it is necessary to stop to take effective and proper observation - near 'blind bends' or the brow of a hill.

3.3 SUMMARY : Making normal stops

* Check the **mirror(s)** : decide if it is safe to carry out your manoeuvre.

* **Signal** if necessary : will it benefit any other road user (including pedestrians)?

* **Manoeuvre** to a parked position : gently braking to a stop.

* When stopped, apply the hand brake and select neutral.

* When stopping to park make sure you choose somewhere that is safe, convenient and legal. Common-sense and your knowledge of the Highway Code will help you to select a suitable place.

4

MAKING EFFECTIVE USE OF MIRRORS

4.1 Properly adjusted . . .

In order that you can make effective use of the mirrors, they must be properly adjusted, clean and clear. (See previous chapter reference adjusting mirrors to suit.)
Remember if you are driving a car used by others, you will need to adjust the mirrors each time you use the car. Also, pedestrians or other road users may have knocked your door/wing mirrors out of alignment - so check **before** you drive away!

Ensure that you know how to adjust all of the mirrors yourself, including the nearside (passenger) door mirror. After all, when you are driving unaccompanied, or on your test, you would have to do it yourself, so make sure you know how!

4.2 "Move your mirror for the examiner . . ."

There is a popular belief that for your driving test you should adjust your mirror so that the examiner can see that you are using the mirror by moving your head. This is absolutely not necessary!!

You should be able to check the mirror with eye movements from your normal seating position.

Should the examiner need to know if you are using the mirror he will usually turn to watch you.

Remember, it is not how many times you look in the mirror that count, but that you make **effective** use of the mirrors. This means that you act sensibly on what you see.

4.3 What your mirrors tell you . . .

Using your mirrors you will know:

*   What type of traffic is behind you? (i.e. cars, vans, motorcycles, lorries, buses, etc).

How close are they, what might they do?

Is it safe to make your manoeuvre?

You will also know:

*   What is behind to judge when it is safe to make your move.

Whether you need to give a signal to help drivers behind you.

4.4 When to use your mirrors . . .

There are certain times when it is vital to check your mirrors:

Well before
i) **D** irection: before changing direction (turning a bend or corner, changing lanes, altering course)

ii) **O** vertaking: Before overtaking

iii) **S** lowing down or stopping: before taking your foot off the gas, or braking

iv) **S** ignalling: before signalling by direction indicator or by arm.

The initials **D.O.S.S.** might help you to remember the specific times above, when your actions could affect other road users.

Apart from the specific times mentioned, check mirrors about every 5 seconds. In busy areas check even more often; remember that the traffic situation can literally change second by second, and you need to know what is happening behind you. Frequent quick glances are best; do not peer at the mirror!

4.5 On reflection . . .

The term "mirrors" refers to the interior and also exterior (door or wing mounted) mirrors. It is especially important to check the exterior mirrors before turning right or left, being aware that cyclists or motorcyclists could ride up along either side of your vehicle.

Remember too, that exterior mirrors generally have a 'convex' (slightly curved) surface and the reflected image will be smaller than a 'true-life' image. This could give you a false impression of speed and distance.

Most interior mirrors have an 'anti-dazzle' switch (usually located centrally on the lower edge of the interior mirror). By moving this switch the glare and dazzle from the lights of following vehicles at night is reduced, giving a less stressful and fatiguing journey.

Should the lights of a following vehicle still prove to be dazzling in your mirror, move your head slightly to avoid this, rather than moving the mirror; as you may not remember to reset it.

4.6 SUMMARY : use of mirrors, how and when

* Make sure all mirrors are clean and properly adjusted.

* Make effective use of mirrors: act sensibly on what you see.

* Know when to use the mirrors.

5

THE EMERGENCY STOP

5.1 When? . . .

A child could run off the pavement in front of your car.

This is just one example of when you would need to do an emergency stop, and is the example used on the driving test to set that scene.

5.2 How? . . .

To stop in an emergency you need to bring the vehicle to a stop promptly (as quickly as possible), under control and without locking the wheels or skidding (wheels stop turning and the vehicle will slide).

Steering control must be maintained when braking heavily as in an emergency. This control needs to be maintained so that you can steer around a person or object.

This is the one time when you stop that you do NOT check the mirror before stopping. This is because travelling at 30 mph you are covering 45ft/15m per second, and in the half second (minimum) that it takes to check the mirror you will have travelled another 23 feet which could be crucial. If you have been using your mirrors properly you will have a good idea of what is behind you.

So the sequence for the emergency stop is as follows:

*   Reacting quickly, take your foot off the gas pedal and . . .

*   Brake hard and progressively. A firm pushing movement - do not stamp on the brake.

*   Keep both hands on the steering wheel, increase your grip on the steering wheel and keep b o t h hands on the wheel until your vehicle comes to a complete stop. (You may need to steer to correct a skid or to avoid a person or object.)

*   Just before the vehicle stops, put the clutch down to prevent the engine from stalling.

*   When the vehicle has come to a **complete** stop, apply the handbrake and select neutral.

*   Prepare the car to move away (select 1st gear) and then check over your left and then your right shoulder before moving away. The check over your left shoulder is vital because with an emergency stop you could be stopped in the middle of the road and other road users may try and pass you on the nearside (passenger side) of your vehicle.

5.3 Engine braking ... stability

When doing an emergency stop do not put the clutch pedal down until just before the vehicle stops.

This is because when the clutch is down the vehicle is coasting or 'free-wheeling' and will take longer to stop, especially if travelling downhill. With the clutch pedal up the engine provides additional braking and helps to keep the vehicle stable and on a straight course.

5.4 Wheels locked ...

If you brake too hard the wheels could lock (stop turning) causing the vehicle to slide along the road surface. If this happens, release the pressure on the brake pedal and then re-apply the pressure, pumping the pedal if necessary.

If the back of the vehicle skids and swings out to the left, steer to the left (into the skid) and get the vehicle back onto a straight course.

When braking hard the vehicle will slide when the adhesion (grip) between the tyre and the road surface is broken.

This grip will be lessened by the following factors:

Condition of road surface:
Loose gravel
Wet leaves
Mud
Oil

Weather conditions which will affect the road surface:
Rain
Ice
Snow
Black Ice (glazed frost)

If any of the above conditions occur take particular care and brake less harshly.

Remember that if the vehicle skids or slides you will have very little or no control.

When the wheels lock the steering wheel will not have any effect and you will not be able to steer around a person or object to avoid them.

It is therefore vital that you do not lock the wheels so that you can maintain control of the steering and therefore the direction of the vehicle.

5.5 ABS Brakes ...

More and more vehicles are now being fitted with ABS (Anti-lock Braking System). This is a device which prevents the wheels from locking, giving maximum braking efficiency. The brakes are at their most effective just before the wheels lock.

The ABS works by sensing electronically when the wheels are about to lock and, a fraction of a second before they do, releasing the brakes. In one second the sensor may release and re-apply the brakes many times. Because the wheels do not ever lock, steering control is maintained, enabling you to steer out of any danger.

When braking heavily (as in an emergency) in a vehicle fitted with ABS you will experience a 'shuddering' sensation as the vehicle stops. This is due to the effect of the brakes being released and re-applied many times very quickly.

Before driving a vehicle you are unfamiliar with check with the handbook or vehicle's owner as to whether it is fitted with ABS.

Anti-lock brakes will NOT prevent you from having an accident, so do not think you can travel closer to other vehicles or reduce your safety margins in any way. Do not be lulled into a false sense of security.

5.6 SUMMARY : emergency stop

* Quick reaction

* Stop under control without locking the wheel or skidding.

* Take effective observation before moving away; check over both left and right shoulders.

6
GIVING APPROPRIATE SIGNALS IN A CLEAR AND UNMISTAKABLE MANNER

6.1 How to give signals ...

There are basic signals that a driver can and should give to help or warn other road users.

These signals are given by:
    Direction indicators
    Brake lights
    Arm signals
    Flashing headlamps
    The horn

6.2 When to signal ...

Signals must be given in good time and for long enough for other road users to see them (or hear, in the case of the horn) and react to them.

Note: A signal does **not** give you the right of way - you must make sure it is safe before carrying out the manoeuvre for which you are signalling.

Do not signal too early; this could be confusing if there are several turnings close together.

Give signals in good time but watch out for situations which call for special care and timing. Also, ensure that you cancel your signals once your manoeuvre has been com-pleted. Failure to do so could confuse and possibly cause danger. When moving away from the kerb, or pulling up at the kerb, it is not necessary to signal if there are clearly no other road users or pedestrians anywhere around.

Remember that it is not just traffic from behind that needs to be considered, but oncoming traffic, cyclists and pedestrians. Before signalling to move away think to yourself 'Will my signal help or warn anyone?'

Do not signal automatically 'just in case I haven't seen anyone'. It is up to you to take proper observation before moving away.

Automatically giving a right turn signal (when moving away from the kerb) without checking could be dangerous: a vehicle (or cyclist) coming from behind might think that you are going to pull away and swerve or brake to avoid you; this could then affect following traffic - causing them to brake or swerve ...

This process of assessing the situation and then making a decision is one that you should develop in all driving tasks - do not act automatically, but think first and then decide the appropriate course of action, consider all prevailing circumstances. Remember that traffic situations change constantly, literally second by second.

When turning into or out of a road you must **always** signal. It is vital to use the correct signal (i.e. if turning left make sure you signal left) and make sure that what you intend to do is safe by using your mirrors first: MIRROR/SIGNAL/MANOEUVRE.

6.3 What the signals mean ...

Direction Indicators:
Usually located on a stalk on the right or left hand side of the steering column; bear in mind that there is no standardised placement of this stalk, so make sure you know which side it is on otherwise you will be switching on the windscreen wipers when you mean to indicate, and vice versa. Particularly important to check if you drive different cars.

The direction indicator stalk is usually placed so that you can operate it with your fingertips whilst keeping both hands on the steering wheel (thereby retaining full control of the vehicle).

Move the direction indication stalk the same way that you would turn the steering wheel: i.e. if you want to signal left move the stalk to the left, and vice versa to turn right.

6.4 Direction Indicator signal right means:

I intend to move out to the right (examples: moving away from the kerb, changing lanes, overtaking, passing a stationary obstruction) or turn right (examples: turning into a road, into a petrol station, into premises).

6.5 Direction Indicator signal left means:

(i)   I intend to move in to the left (example: changing lanes).

(ii)   I intend to turn left (examples: turning into road, into a petrol station, into premises).

(iii) I intend to stop on the left (example: pulling up by the kerb). Be especially careful when stopping on the left before a left turn; in this situation an additional signal by arm (I intend to slow down or stop) would clarify your intention.

6.6 Brake lights

Brake lights help and warn other road users by showing that you are slowing down or stopping.

The brake lights are activated when you press the foot-brake pedal. They do not activate when the handbrake is used. The brake lights are two bright red lights at the rear of the vehicle.

Be aware that from the time you realise you need to use the brakes to the moment the brake lights come on there is a time-lag. This is called the thinking distance. There is also a certain amount of free travel of the brake pedal before it activates the brake lights.

Because of these factors it is advisable to brake earlier to give following traffic more time to see and react to your signals; you will stop more smoothly as well.

6.7 Arm signals ...

Please note that arm signals mean just that - use of the full length of the arm, not hands or fingers waving uselessly out of barely opened window!

Up until the mid 1970s driving test candidates would be instructed to use only arm signals (not direction indicators) for a period of time during the test. Although this no longer applies you will be expected to know how, and when, to use arm signals. And you could be asked to demonstrate them during the questions on the highway code and other motoring matters at the end of the practical (driving) part of the test.

Arm signals would need to be used:

* if the direction indicators failed.

* to reinforce and clarify direction indicator signals and stop lights.

You also need to know the meaning of arm signals because they may be used by other road users such as:

* Cyclists/motor cyclists
* Horse riders
* Other drivers

Arm signals can also be used to indicate your intentions to a person controlling the traffic: uniformed police officer, traffic warden, school crossing patrol.
The Highway Code illustrates all arm signals, giving their precise meaning.

6.8 "Do I need to give arm signals"?

There is one situation in which an arm signal **should** be used; when you are the driver of the first vehicle approaching a zebra (uncontrolled) pedestrian crossing.

The arm signal used would be the slowing down or stopping signal. This helps and warns the following road users:

* Pedestrians waiting to cross.

* Traffic behind you (an arm signal is visible to more than brake lights, which are only seen by the vehicle immediately behind).

* Oncoming traffic (your arm signal will inform them that you are slowing down or stopping and could well influence them to stop).

Use this signal if you have time (remember that you will need to open your window first!) and, if you are the first vehicle to approach, the sequence to use is:
Mirror

Mirror
Signal
(arm signal and brake lights)
Manoeuvre
(gently braking to stop)

As a guideline this arm signal should be given for as long as it takes you to slowly say "I am slowing down and stopping".

6.9 Arm signals and how to give them.

*   Open window fully, right arm outstretched, palm facing forward.

I intend to move out to the right or turn right.

*   Open window fully, right arm outstretched, palm facing the ground, rotate your arm slowly in an anti-clockwise direction.

I intend to move into the left or turn left.

*   Open window fully, right arm out stretched, palm facing the ground, move arm slowly up and down.

I intend to slow down or stop.

6.10 Headlamp flashing

Use only as a warning of your presence to other road users.

Make sure you give a positive signal say for a count of 3 seconds, slowly say to yourself "one second, two seconds, three seconds".

Use the headlamp flash when a horn signal would not be suitable or appropriate; for example, on a road with a high noise level (dual carriageway/motorway), or at dusk/night-time on a road with 'blind' bends (where you cannot see approaching traffic).

Do not use headlamp flashing for any other reasons; it could be misinterpreted with dangerous consequences.

6.11 Horn signals

The horn is a warning instrument to give other road users an audible signal to make them aware of your presence. Do not use the horn angrily as a rebuke to other road users.

Some examples of when you would need to use the horn:

* Before 'blind' bends

* Before a 'blind' brow of a hill

* If a pedestrian is going to step into the road and has not looked.

* If a vehicle is reversing into a road (from a driveway) and is not aware of your presence.

When using the horn consider the length of note to give.

For pedestrians a short 'tap' on the horn may be sufficient; a longer note could startle or alarm them, especially young children and old people.

For cyclists a short 'tap' will also suffice; if they were startled by a longer note they could swerve or wobble, causing danger to themselves and others.

For vehicles a longer note should be sounded; a driver is insulated from external noise to a certain extent and also he may have the radio or tape player on, or even be on the phone.

There are certain restrictions on the use of the horn:

(i) Do not use when the vehicle is stationary, except at times of danger due to another vehicle moving.

(ii) In a built-up area do not use the horn between 11.30 p.m. and 7.00 a.m.

NOTE: Some anti-theft devices which are fitted to vehicles will sound the horn or a klaxon when there is attempted theft of, or from, the vehicle. This is a legal exception to the above mentioned restriction on stationary vehicles.

6.12 Signals given by other road users

Be aware that other drivers may signal to you in various situations using a variety of methods.

For example if you are waiting to join a busy main road on which heavy traffic is moving slowly, another driver may indicate to you that he is letting you in. He could do this by:

Flashing his headlamps
Beckoning with hand or arm movement
Head movement
Eye movement
Raising eyebrows

In a situation as described above it is important to make eye contact (look the driver in the eye to let him know that you have seen him) with a driver who might let you in. Eye contact will let you know that he has seen you, and then watch for another signal (as above) to indicate that he will let you join the traffic flow. Also by watching carefully you will be certain to see any given signal; in traffic situations where this may apply drivers are usually being held up and in a frame of mind where, should you not react quickly to a signal, they could then deliberately block or hinder someone else out of frustration and annoyance; an angry driver is a dangerous driver!

However, it is up to you to make sure it is safe before you act on other's signals.

Consider all possibilities: they may be unaware of cyclists or motor cyclists coming from behind on either side. They may even be signalling to someone else.

6.13 Signals given by emergency vehicles

Vehicles with flashing lights/sirens will be:

Blue flashing light:
Police
Fire Brigade
Ambulance
Salvage Corps
Forestry Commission
Fire Dpt.
Blood Transfusion
H.M. Coastguard
NCB Mine Rescue
Bomb Disposal
RAF Mountain Rescue
RNLI Vehicles
Vehicles dealing with nuclear accident/radioactivity

Green flashing light:
Doctor

Amber flashing light:
Road Clearance
Breakdown Vehicles
Road Maintenance/Cleaning

Note: Police and ambulance vehicles do not always use flashing blue lights and two-tone sirens. They could use only flashing blue lights. By using mirrors properly you will be aware of any such emergency vehicles.

Always endeavour to leave a way clear for them - pulling in to the side of the road, etc. Do not hinder them in any way.

6.14 SUMMARY - Giving appropriate signals in a clear and unmistakable manner

* Give signals where necessary

* Correctly

* Properly timed

* Different methods of signalling:

Direction indicators
   Brake lights
   Arm signals
   Horn signals
   Headlamp flashing

Where, when and how.

* Signals given by other road users and how to act on them.

7

GENERAL ROAD POSITIONING

7.1 Drive on the left . . .

In the U.K. we drive on the left. Historically this dates from the times of horse travel. By keeping to the left a horseman could wield a sword or pistol in his right hand, thereby protecting himself, (or attacking) with his strongest hand. Obviously nowadays we do not use swords or pistols but the habit of keeping to the left has remained.

7.2 Normal driving position

Your normal driving position should be 3ft/1m from the nearside (passenger side) kerb, where road and traffic conditions allow. Obviously in a narrow road you will not be able to give 3ft/1m clearance, but whatever the clearance, keep that distance constant and do not weave in and out.

If you are passing a line of parked vehicles do not move in and out of any gaps there may be but drive in a line which keeps you clear of the parked vehicles.

Allow parked vehicles a clearance of approximately a door's width.

Do not drive on the crown (middle) of the road - it does not allow sufficient clearance to oncoming vehicles.

Do not drive in the gutter - it puts you too close to the kerb and to any pedestrians who may be on the pavement. Also the road surface is likely to be pot-holed or broken up and there may be drain covers or gratings. All of these things could either cause damage to your tyres or else cause you to change direction, possibly veering into the kerb.

7.3 Position for turning

When turning left, or going straight ahead, keep to your normal driving position.

If you are turning right keep just to the left of the centre of the road. If there is no centre line marking you will have to imagine where the centre of the road is.

If you are turning right out of a narrow road (either physically narrow or narrowed with parked vehicles/obstructions) position yourself well to the left; this will allow room for any vehicles wishing to enter the road you are turning out of.

7.4 Position when driving in lanes

When driving in lanes, position the vehicle in the middle of the lane; do not straddle lane lines as this may force other vehicles to form new lanes causing a potentially dangerous situation.

On dual carriageways and motorways keep to the left-hand lane: you may drive in the centre lane when overtaking or if there are slower vehicles in the left-hand lane. However, you should return to the left-hand lane as soon as you can but without cutting in.

The extreme right-hand lane is used for overtaking only.

7.5 Position in bends

For both right-hand and left-hand bends keep well to the left. This will give you greater clearance of oncoming traffic which may be travelling over the central lines.

Right-hand bend
From your position well to the left you will have a very good view into and possibly through the bend. However, do not let this tempt you to enter or drive through the bend at a higher speed.

Left-hand bend
Your view in this situation will be restricted, so take particular care and consider possible hazards; vehicles parked or broken down, animals on the road (horses for example) slower road users (cyclists) or even pedestrians. Take special care on country roads.

7.6 Position in one-way streets

In one-way streets your position will depend on whether you are going straight ahead, turning left or turning right.

Turning Left: Keep to the left

Turning Right: Keep to the right

Straight ahead: Watch for road markings/keep to the left.

If there are only two lanes, make your choice and stay in lane.

Be aware that in a one-way street traffic may overtake on the left (when safe).

7.7 SUMMARY:
general road positioning

* Do not drive in the middle of the road.

* Do not drive in the gutter.

* Know your 'normal' driving position.

* Correct positioning in bends and one-way streets.

You are entirely responsible for the vehicle being in the correct position on the road; by doing this you will fit into the traffic flow causing the least trouble to other road users.

8

SPEED

8.1 How fast? . . .

Speed in itself is not dangerous, but in the wrong situation and under certain circumstances it can be LETHAL.

Care must be taken to ensure that the speed you drive at is suitable for the road and traffic conditions and that you **exercise care in the use of speed.**

This means being prepared to slow down or keep your speed down as necessary (recognising hazards and adjusting speed to suit).

Do not let your speed change for no reason. This will only confuse and alarm other road users. Try to get the 'feel' of the car at 30 mph etc., so that you do not have to constantly refer to the speedometer. Remember it is vital that you keep your eyes on the road whenever possible. By planning ahead and anticipating you will be able to adjust your speed in good time for any hazard or new speed limit.

8.2 How slow? . . .

Driving too slowly can cause problems for other road users - you could hinder them causing drivers to become annoyed and frustrated.

This in turn could lead them to overtake when it was unsafe or dangerous.

8.3 What speed do I drive at?

Drive at a speed which keeps you moving with the traffic flow, where possible.

This is called making normal progress. Make sure you build up speed quickly between gears, and if the road is clear then drive briskly and smoothly.

As a rough guide it should take approximately 10 seconds for you to reach 30 mph on a level road from rest.

The speed you drive at will be determined by:

(i) the distance you can see to be clear;

(ii) the speed limits in force;

(iii) road, traffic and weather conditions.

(i) The distance you can see to be clear

Consider minimum stopping distances - ask yourself "could I stop in time". Take particular care at night - make sure that you can stop in the distance you can see to be shown clear by your headlights.

(ii) The speed limits in force

* **30 mph** -   built-up area
* **60 mph** -   single carriageway
* **70 mph** -   dual carriageway / motorway
  Unless signposted lower

Remember these are maximum speeds and you need to take into account:

(iii) Road conditions

Consider the road surface -
  loose gravel
  road works
  surface worn smooth

Traffic conditions

How much moving traffic, consider parked vehicles (road width narrowed).

Weather conditions

Rain/ice/snow will affect your visibility (impairs vision through windows and mirrors). Slow down! Give yourself more time to stop!

8.4 When clear . . .

When the road is clear drive briskly and smoothly to as near the speed limit as road, traffic and weather conditions allow. Where necessary adjust your speed to suit the conditions.

When making normal progress you will fit in with the traffic flow without causing any undue delay to other road users. This also means not being hesitant at any junctions or point where traffic meets or joins.

8.5 Stopping Distance, Including between your ears . . .

Make sure you know your stopping distances.

The distance a vehicle will travel from the moment you realise you must brake to the moment the vehicle stops is called the overall stopping distance. The overall stopping distance is made up of:

* Thinking distance   *   Braking distance.

SPEED (MPH)	THINKING DISTANCE		BRAKING DISTANCE		OVERALL STOPPING DISTANCE	
	Ft	M	Ft	M	Ft	M
20	20	6	20	6	40	12
30	30	9	45	14	75	23
40	40	12	80	24	120	36
50	50	15	125	38	175	53
60	60	18	180	55	240	73
70	70	21	245	75	315	96
80	80	24	320	97	400	121
90	90	27	405	123	495	150
100	100	30	500	151	600	180

The thinking distance is calculated at 7/10ths of a second. (Research has shown this to be the average reaction time.)

For example a vehicle travelling at 50 mph is covering 75 feet per second and, therefore in 7/10th of a second will have travelled 52.5 feet. (Figures are rounded to the nearest number for the table).

The stopping distance will be affected by:

a) condition of road surface (wet, loose gravel, etc.)

b) the state of your health (physical and mental fitness).

c) condition of your brakes and tyres.

d) whether you are travelling on a level road, uphill (shorter stopping distance) or downhill (longers t o p - ping distance).

It is one thing to know the stopping distances, but quite another to actually be able to judge distances accurately on the road.

There are various formulae for working out the stopping distances but in reality, out on the road, by the time you have worked out your distance you would have crashed into the vehicle in front!

An experiment you can try as a pedestrian to get the 'feel' of distance is to pick an object and estimate its distance. Then pace it out (one large stride per metre) and see how close your estimate was.

If you relate the stopping distances to car lengths, i.e. 120 feet is 10 car lengths, it might help you to get a better idea of distance.

Really the only thing to help you is the distance between your ears - your brain - and use this to consider:

* The speed you are travelling at?

* What are the conditions?

* How alert is the driver?

* Condition of the car (brakes, tyres, etc.)?

* Uphill/downhill?

At speeds of 40 mph and over the '2 second rule' can be used to ensure that you travel at a safe distance behind the vehicle in front of you.

The way this works is as follows:

When the vehicle in front of you passes a fixed point (lamp-post, bridge, etc.) count 1 second 2 seconds by saying it to yourself slowly. If you reach the same fixed point before you have finished saying 1 second, 2 seconds, then you are too close and should slow down to increase the gap.

Travelling at 50 mph you are covering 75 feet per second, therefore in 2 seconds you will have travelled 150 feet which is approximately the overall stopping distance.

At speeds below 40 mph the 2 second rule does not work because a 2 second gap would give unrealistically large spacing between vehicles - especially in a built-up area - and other road users would continually be moving into that space causing you to constantly slow down - this in turn can cause frustration and anger in the following road users.

The following table relates your speed in miles per hour to your speed in feet/metres per second (approximately, speed + 50% = feet per second).

20 mph =	30ft/10m
30 mph =	45ft/15m
40 mph =	60ft/20m
50 mph =	75ft/25m
60 mph =	90ft/30m
70 mph =	105ft/35m
80 mph =	120ft/40m
90 mph =	135ft/45m
100 mph =	150ft/50m

8.5 SUMMARY : speed

* Exercise proper care in use of speed.

* Make normal progress.

* Know the speed limits.

    Speed: MPH.

    Consider in feet per second.

    Read the road ahead.

    Anticipate.

9.1 How to . . .

The most important thing about approaching and turning corners is to be at the correct speed and in the most appropriate gear.

Your road speed at a corner will depend on how sharp the corner is and whether there are other road users about (consider drivers, cyclists and pedestrians).

By using a set procedure or system on approach to a corner, you are safely able to consider the hazard and assess it, and act accordingly, all in good time.

9.2 System of Approach

In chapter 4 the mirror/signal/manoeuvre routine was discussed, and it is this same procedure (extended) that is used when approaching and turning corners.

The system is extended as follows:

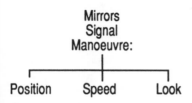

Mirrors
Signal
Manoeuvre:

Position   Speed   Look

As you will see the manoeuvre part is divided into 3 elements: **position/speed/look.**

So the system can now be called **MSPSL:**

> **Mirrors**
> **Signal**
> **Position**
> **Speed**
> **Look**

The following examples detail precisely each part of the manoeuvre.

9.3 Turning left
(major road into minor road)

Level road:

Mirrors: Check for position and speed of following traffic.

Signal: Indicate left.

Position: Normal driving position/constant distance from kerb - do not veer into the kerb or veer out (this could cause danger to overtaking vehicles and/or oncoming traffic). Maintain a constant distance from the kerb or parked vehicles on left.

Speed: Reduce your speed with your brakes. The foot-brake is the most efficient method of slowing the vehicle. Also, when the brake pedal is pressed the brake lights will light up, telling following traffic that you are slowing down. (Remember: gears for go, brakes for slow). When you have reduced speed for the corner, select the appropriate gear which will generally be 2nd gear (for sharper corners or restricted view, use 1st). The vehicle should be at its lowest speed just before you start to turn the corner.

From that point on the vehicle should be **driven** around the corner at a **steady speed**. To do this your right foot would need to be gently pressing the gas pedal so that the vehicle is neither speeding up nor slowing down, but travelling at a constant speed.

It is important to drive around corners at a steady speed because this will cause the vehicle to be **most stable, and balanced**, with the vehicle's weight being evenly distributed over all four wheels. However, if the brakes were applied this would shift the weight forward on to the front wheels causing the vehicle to be less stable.

Similarly if the vehicle was accelerated when turning the corner the vehicle's weight would be shifted towards the rear, again giving less stability.

So, when approaching and turning corners all necessary braking and gear changing must be done **before** you actually turn, ensuring that you have both hands on the wheel and the vehicle's speed is under control.

When approaching corners **do not coast** (clutch held down) as this can cause the vehicle to speed up (especially if travelling downhill).

Look: Before turning into your new road, look ahead to make sure no-one is cutting across your path, also look into the new road and make sure you can enter it safely.
Consider:

* **Any pedestrians crossing the road?**
(They have right of way when crossing).

* **Is the road clear?**
(It is up to you to make sure you can enter the road - vehicles already in that road have priority).

Also before turning left check your nearside (passenger) door mirror for any cyclists. Do not overtake cyclists just before turning left or motorcyclists which may come up on your nearside (passenger side).

When you enter your new road take up your normal driving position and when your vehicle is on a straight course check your mirror (assess situation behind) and if safe (i.e. no vehicle preparing to overtake you) more gas, accelerate briskly and smoothly.

The above procedure would apply if the road was level (not uphill or downhill). Please note the following changes when approaching and turning corners when travelling uphill or downhill.

9.4 Turning left (major road into minor road)

Uphill gradient

Sequence as above: mirror/signal/position/speed/look.

However, consider how steep the gradient is; by taking your foot off the gas pedal the car will slow down due to the effects of gravity and you may need only to use the brakes very slightly to reduce speed for the corner, or to warn following traffic (brake lights). eg slightly to reduce speed for the corner, or to warn following traffic (brake lights).

Then select the most appropriate gear (generally 2nd gear, but consider how sharp the corner is and if there are any other road users about). Select the gear in good time, so that your left foot comes up off the clutch pedal and your left hand is back on the steering wheel so that you can concentrate on controlling the vehicle when steering it around the corner.

You should then drive the vehicle around the corner, with your right foot pressing gently on the gas pedal so that you travel around the corner at a steady speed.

Remember, when approaching and turning corners do not coast (clutch held down) as this can lessen the amount of control you have over the vehicle.

When you enter your new road take up your normal driving position and when your vehicle is on a straight course (i.e. you have completed the turn and the vehicle is travelling parallel to the kerb) check your mirrors to assess the situation behind and, if safe (i.e. no vehicle preparing to overtake you), accelerate briskly and smoothly.

9.5 Turning left (major road into minor road)

Downhill gradient

Sequence as before: mirror/signal/position/speed/look.

However, consider the gradient and remember that due to the effect of gravity you will need more braking effort to slow the vehicle down, so start your braking earlier.

When turning a corner on a downhill gradient it will usually be necessary to be gently pressing on the **brake** as you turn in order to maintain a steady speed.

Remember, when approaching and turning corners do not coast (clutch held down) as this can cause the vehicle to speed up, especially when travelling downhill. This is because with the clutch dis-engaged there is no engine braking.

Having covered in detail approaching and turning into a side road, the following would apply when turning right from a major road into a minor road (main road into side road).

APPROACHING AND TURNING CORNERS
TURNING LEFT

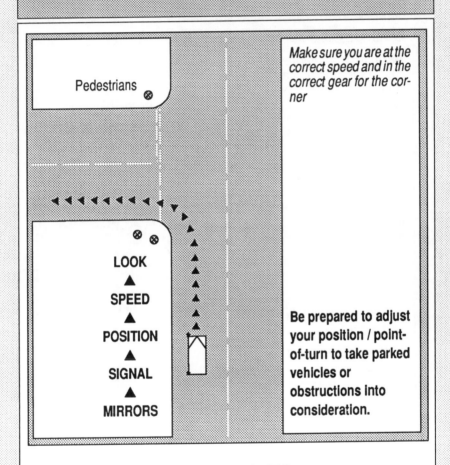

Pedestrians

Make sure you are at the correct speed and in the correct gear for the corner

LOOK
▲
SPEED
▲
POSITION
▲
SIGNAL
▲
MIRRORS

Be prepared to adjust your position / point-of-turn to take parked vehicles or obstructions into consideration.

SAFETY FACTORS

* Do not coast on approach or while turning
* Do not veer in or out on approach
* Regulate speed correctly on approach
* Give way when turning to pedestrians who are crossing

APPROACHING AND TURNING CORNERS
TURNING RIGHT

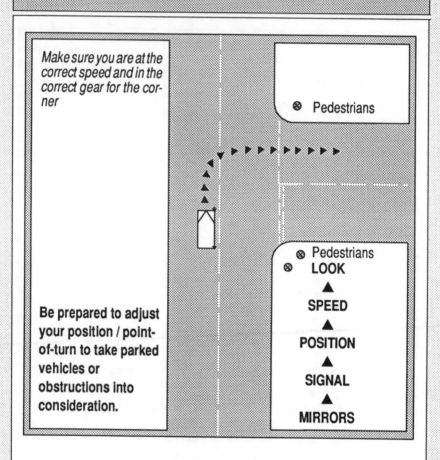

Make sure you are at the correct speed and in the correct gear for the corner

⊗ Pedestrians

Be prepared to adjust your position / point-of-turn to take parked vehicles or obstructions into consideration.

⊗ Pedestrians
⊗ **LOOK**
▲
SPEED
▲
POSITION
▲
SIGNAL
▲
MIRRORS

SAFETY FACTORS

* Do not coast on approach or while turning
* Do not veer in or out on approach
* Regulate speed correctly on approach
* Give way when turning to pedestrians who are crossing

9.6 Turning right (major road into minor road)

Level Road

The sequence on approach is as follows:

Mirrors: Check for position and speed of following traffic and make sure it is safe to carry out your manoeuvre.

Signal: Indicate right.

Position: Your correct position for turning right should be just left of the centre of the road. Central white line markings may help you, or you will have to assess where the centre of the road is.

Speed: Reduce your speed with your brakes. The foot-brake is the most efficient method of slowing the vehicle. Also, when the brake pedal is pressed the brake lights will light up, telling following traffic that you are slowing down. (Remember: gears for go, brakes for slow.) When you have reduced speed for the corner, select the appropriate gear which will generally be 2nd gear (for sharper corners or restricted view, use 1st). The vehicle should be at its lowest speed just before you start to turn the corner.

From that point on the vehicle should be **driven** around the corner at a **steady speed.** To do this your right foot would need to be gently pressing the gas pedal so that the vehicle is neither speeding up nor slowing down, but travelling at a constant speed.

It is important to drive around corners at a steady speed because this will cause the vehicle to be **most stable, and balanced,** with the vehicle's weight being evenly distributed over all four wheels. However, if the brakes were applied this would shift the weight forward on to the front wheels causing the vehicle to be less stable.

Similarly if the vehicle was accelerated when turning the corner the vehicle's weight would be shifted towards the rear, again giving less stability.

So, when approaching and turning corners all necessary braking and gear changing must be done **before** you actually turn, ensuring that you have both hands on the wheel and the vehicle's speed is under control.

When approaching corners **do not coast** (clutch held down) as this can cause the vehicle to speed up (especially if travelling downhill).

Look: Before turning into your new road look ahead, give way to oncoming traffic and before you cross the path of oncoming traffic make sure you can do so **without causing them to change their speed** (brake or slow down) **or direction** (swerve or change course).

If you did make oncoming traffic change their speed or direction it could be extremely dangerous; vehicles braking could cause following traffic to brake. Also if you caused vehicles to swerve to avoid you it could cause them to crash into traffic going the other way.

When in this situation of crossing the path of oncoming traffic you may find it difficult to judge when it is safe to go.

As a guideline, ask yourself if you could walk across without causing oncoming traffic to change their speed or direction. If you could walk across, you could drive across! After all, as a pedestrian you are assessing and making decisions like that each time you cross the road. As a driver this will come with experience and practice. All the time that you are learning to drive you will have an accompanying driver with you who can advise when it is safe to go or not.

Make sure that, when you cross the path of approaching traffic, the back of your car is **completely** in the new road before any traffic passes. This will ensure an adequate safety margin between your vehicle and passing traffic. If you have not fully completed your turn you could cause traffic to brake or swerve to avoid you.

Having decided you can cross safely, check your mirrors again (especially offside [driver's side] mirror in case of cyclists or motorcyclists attempting to overtake) and also ensure that you can enter your new road. Consider:

* Any pedestrians crossing - remember they have right of way when crossing.

* Is the road clear - remember it is up to **you** to make sure you can enter the road. Vehicles in the road have priority as they are already there. If you entered the road and it wasn't clear you could be forced to reverse out into the main road - both illegal and very dangerous.

When turning right from a main road into a side road avoid 'cutting the corner'. This is dangerous because it reduces your view of any traffic in the road and it also puts you on the wrong side of the road.

If you start to turn too early you will cut the corner. The correct point-of-turn is when the front of your vehicle is level with the middle of the road you are turning into. You should make a neat 90 degrees (right angle) turn. If (because of oncoming traffic in the major road) you have to stop and wait, ensure that the front of your vehicle is about 1 yard/metre **before** the middle of the road into which you are turning. This is because when you are stationary you must not turn the steering wheel (it could damage the steering mechanism). Therefore you will use the 1 metre/yard to move forward into so that you can move the steering wheel to make the turn.

Do not edge forward whilst you are waiting - this could cause you to turn wide, possibly inviting a following vehicle to 'cut' inside you to make the same turn.

When you are in your new road and on a straight course, check your mirrors and if safe (make sure no vehicles are preparing to overtake) accelerate briskly and smoothly.

9.7 Turning right (major road into minor road)

Uphill gradient

Sequence as before: mirror/signal/position/speed/look.

However, consider how steep the gradient is. By taking your foot off the gas pedal the car will slow down due to the effects of gravity and you may need only to use the brakes very slightly to reduce speed for the corner, or to warn following traffic.

Then select the most appropriate gear (generally 2nd gear, but consider how sharp the corner is and if there are any other road users about).

Having selected the most appropriate gear you should then drive the vehicle around the corner, with your right foot pressing gently on the gas pedal so that you travel around the corner at a steady speed.

Remember, when approaching and turning corners do not coast (clutch held down) as this can cause the vehicle to speed up, especially when travelling downhill.

When you enter your new road take up your normal driving position and when your vehicle is on a straight course (i.e. you have completed the turn and the vehicle is travelling parallel to the kerb) check your mirrors to assess the situation behind, if safe (i.e. no vehicle preparing to overtake you), accelerate briskly and smoothly.

9.8 Turning right (major road into minor road)

Downhill gradient

Sequence as before: mirror/signal/position/speed/look.

However, consider the gradient and remember that you will need more braking effort to slow the vehicle down, so start your braking earlier.

When turning a corner on a downhill gradient it will usually be necessary to be gently pressing on the **brake** as you turn in order to maintain a steady speed.

Remember, when approaching and turning corners do not coast (clutch held down) as this can cause the vehicle to speed up, especially when travelling downhill.

9.9 What about parked vehicles. ?

With so much traffic on the roads there will usually be parked vehicles or obstructions (builders skips, roadworks, etc.) both in the main road and on the side road into which you are turning.

Parked vehicles and other obstructions will affect you in the following way:-

* By reducing the available road width.

* By restricting your view of the road and other road users.

First, we will consider the left turn, major road to minor road with parked vehicles or obstructions.

9.10 Left turn (parked vehicles)

Sequence as before: mirror/signal/position/speed/look.

However, you should adjust your position to take into account parked vehicles on the left, and maintain a position that allows you adequate clearance (a door's width, 1m/1yd) and maintain a constant distance from those parked vehicles.

As you approach the corner look into your new road - any parked vehicles or obstructions will reduce the road width and may obscure your view - drive at a speed that you can stop safely if necessary and assume there is a vehicle coming down the road - remember that they have priority - it is up to you to check and make sure it is safe to enter your new road. Also, if there are roadworks vehicles, assume there will be workmen around and be alert to sudden pedestrian movements in and around the road-works.

9.11 Right turn (parked vehicles)

Sequence as before: mirror/signal/position/speed/look.

When positioning the vehicle to turn right take into account parked vehicles on both sides of the road and adjust your position accordingly.

Remember that any vehicles parked on the right hand side of the road will narrow the road width, and if you were to take up a position just left of the centre of the road it could put you on a collision course with oncoming traffic. What you should do is to assess the available road width, that is the distance from one kerb or obstruction to the obstruction on the other side and decide where the middle of that new width is and position your vehicle just left of that. In some instances you may have to position your vehicle even further left - assess and make your decision taking all prevailing factors into account.

If the road you are turning into has parked vehicles or obstructions (builders skips, roadworks, etc.) you should consider the following:

* How much can you see?

* By how much is the road width reduced?

* Is there traffic already in the road?

9.12 New road (parked vehicles on left)

If there are parked vehicles or obstructions on the **left-hand side** of the road you are turning into you should assess the available width and judge where the middle of that width is; this will be the new point-of-turn. Because you will now start turning earlier you could find that you will be 'cutting the corner'. In this situation it is acceptable. However, you must make **absolutely** sure that you can enter the road safely. This means looking into the road (any traffic coming down?) and deciding that you will not inconvenience or endanger other road users.

9.13 New road (parked vehicles on right)

If there are any parked vehicles or obstructions on the right-hand side of the road you are turning into you should consider how this will affect you. Obviously the road width will be narrowed and because of this any traffic coming down the road could be positioned further over, on your side of the road, so be prepared to adjust your position by moving further over to the left.

As above, ensure that you look properly into the road **before** committing yourself to the turn.

9.14 New road (parked vehicles both sides)

Obviously this will severely reduce the available width of road and particular care must be taken under these circumstances. Do not enter the road until it is completely safe to do so. In these conditions it may be possible for only one lane of traffic to be in the road at any one time. If there is oncoming traffic in a severely narrowed road then they have priority - they are already in the road and obviously cannot easily change their position or direction to accommodate you.

It is up to you to ensure that you **look properly** into the road **before** turning into it.

9.15 Approaching and driving around bends

A bend is defined as a change in the direction of the road but without other roads joining it.

On approaching the bend the sequence is as follows: (for either right or left-hand bends)

Mirrors: Check for following traffic (speed, position, etc.)

Signal: Brake lights will signal to following traffic that you are slowing down.

Position: Well to the left (both right or left-hand bends).

Speed: Reduce speed with your brakes and then select the **most appropriate gear** for the bend.

Look: Look as far ahead as the bend will allow. Depending on the local conditions (trees, hedges, fences, etc.) - you may be able to see 'across' the bend and get earlier warning of any hazards.

On approach to a bend you will be able to make an assessment of how sharp the bend is by using the following method:

*   Notice the point at which the nearside (left-hand) and offside (right-hand) verges meet. This is called the **limit point.**

65

* A bend will be **sharp** if this limit point remains fixed and the view does not improve. Take particular care and consider that there may be hazards (broken down vehicle/pedestrians/slow vehicle, etc.) immediately after the bend.

* The bend will be more **gradual** if the limit point moves away.

Having driven around the bend at a steady speed (to maintain the maximum stability of the vehicle) with your right foot on the gas - enough to keep the speed constant - straighten the vehicle and check your mirror. If safe (no vehicles about to overtake), accelerate briskly and smoothly.

As with approaching and turning corners, do not coast (clutch down) when driving around bends; this reduces your control of the vehicle and can cause the vehicle to speed up (especially travelling downhill).

9.16 SUMMARY - Approaching and turning corners and bends

* Use MSPSL sequence on approach.

* All braking and gear changing is done **before** the bend or corner.

* Always drive around a corner or bend at a steady speed.

* Make sure you look **properly** before entering a new road.

10

DEALING WITH JUNCTIONS

10.1 What is a junction? . . .

A junction is where one or more roads meet, and can vary from a simple T junction to complex road systems.

There are four basic types of junction:

* **Give way**

* **Controlled (traffic light)**

* **Stop**

* **Unmarked**

The majority of junctions are give way junctions.

At a give way junction the 'mouth' of the junction will be marked by double broken white lines on the side of the road you emerge from, and a single broken white line on the side that you would enter the road. There will also be a triangular give way road sign on your side of the road.

The double broken white lines mean give way to traffic on the major road - it is not necessary to come to a complete stop if the road is clear and you can emerge safely.

10.2 Controlled (traffic light) junctions

Controlled (traffic light) junctions help to keep traffic moving and maintain a regular traffic flow at junctions which otherwise may become congested.

The traffic light sequence is as follows:

Colour:	Meaning:
Red	*Stop*
Red with Amber	*Stop*
Green	*Go* (only if the junction is clear)
Steady Amber	*Stop* (unless you have crossed the white stop line or are so close to it that to pull up would cause an accident)

Although controlled junctions make it easier for you by telling you to go or stop you must anticipate signal changes on approach to traffic lights and act accordingly.

Be aware that even when the lights are green for you, there may be vehicles 'jumping' the red lights from the opposite direction. Before driving through a junction, check all other roads for vehicle movements.

10.3 Stop Junctions

Stop junctions are relatively rare and are identified by a solid white stop line on your side of the 'mouth' of the junction and an octagonal red road sign with the word 'stop' on it.

The stop sign is octagonal (eight sided) so that it can be distinguished from the give way sign even if the wording on the sign and the stop line are covered in snow.

At a stop junction you **must** bring the vehicle to a complete stop. The reason for having stop junctions is so that you take effective observation at dangerous junctions.

Stop junctions are located where your view is severely restricted, for example:

*   Near a bend/brow of hill.

*   Where buildings or fences/trees, etc., limit your view.

*   At busy junctions with several roads.

*   At a junction with a main road carrying fast moving traffic.

You must bring your vehicle to a **complete** stop in order that you can take effective observation. If it was a give way junction you might be tempted to emerge without looking

properly, thereby causing danger or inconvenience to other road users.

10.4 Unmarked Junctions

There are relatively few unmarked junctions - however, you must know how to deal with them.

Assume that all the roads have equal priority, proceed with caution and be prepared to give way to other traffic. Consider that they may think they have 'right of way' and will carry on regardless?

If one road is wider or busier than the other it will generally be treated as having priority. However, never assume this and take the utmost care before emerging, crossing or travelling through unmarked junctions.

Having covered the four basic junction types we will now deal with approaching and emerging at junctions.

10.5 Approaching a Junction

On approach to a junction you should check your mirrors and then assess the situation ahead of you and try and get as much advance information as possible.

*   What sort of junction is it? (Stop, give way, etc).

*   How many roads are joining?

* Any other road users about?

* Width of roads.

* Traffic conditions. (How busy?)

* Traffic signs. (Stop, give way, turn left, etc).

As you get nearer to the junction use the mirror/signal/position/speed/look routine (this will be detailed later for emerging and turning left and right).

On approach to the junction regulate your speed so that you do not rush up; this could alarm and confuse other road users. However, do not crawl up to the junction and do not coast (clutch down) as this can make the vehicle travel faster (especially downhill) and gives you less control.

10.6 Taking effective observation

At most junctions visibility is not very good, therefore it is vital that you **take effective observation** before deciding whether to wait or go on.

The observation you must take is:

Look right

Look left

Look right again

This applies for left and right turns from a minor road into a major road. Obviously the immediate danger is from your right. However, it is also vital to check left **before** emerging - there may be pedestrians crossing or even an overtaking vehicle coming towards you on your side of the road.

The observation routine (right/left/right) must be done at least once - at a busy junction you may have to do it many times.

If you are turning left and your view is blocked by a large vehicle turning right do not assume it is safe to go - you have not taken **effective** observation. Consider that there may be a motorcyclist or a car coming around the large vehicle. So, just because the road is blocked do not think it is clear for you to go . . . Be aware of what could happen.

10.7 If your view is restricted . . .

Sometimes at junctions when at the give way lines or kerb line, you will not be able to take effective observation due to any or all of the following:

* Parked vehicles on major road.

* Trees/lamp-posts/post boxes obscuring your view.

* Pedestrians.

* Road-works on major road.

In this situation you must drive the car forward to a point where you can take effective observation. By doing this you will be widening your 'zone of vision' to enable you to look properly.

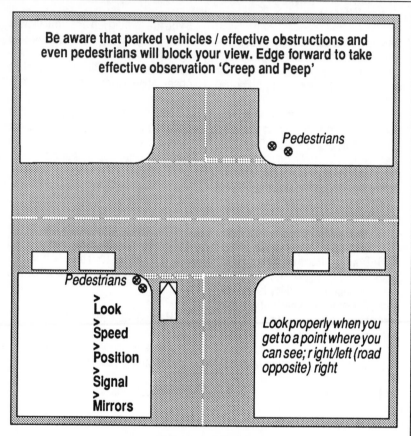

Be aware that parked vehicles / effective obstructions and even pedestrians will block your view. Edge forward to take effective observation 'Creep and Peep'

Pedestrians

Pedestrians

> Look
> Speed
> Position
> Signal
> Mirrors

Look properly when you get to a point where you can see; right/left (road opposite) right

SAFETY FACTORS

* Regulate speed on approach, use gears selectively.
* Do not coast.
* Take effective observation before emerging.
* Emerge with due regard for approaching traffic.
* Give way to pedestrians who are crossing.

The point at which you can take effective observation will be when your **eyes**, not the front of the car, are on a level with the obstacle that is preventing you from seeing.

By physically leaning forward (in your seat) you can widen your zone of vision without necessarily placing your vehicle directly in the traffic flow. However, if by doing this you are still not able to see properly you must edge the vehicle forward slowly to take effective observation.

10.8 Emerging from a junction

When emerging from a junction make sure it is safe: do not make any other road users change speed (brake/slow down) or direction (swerve/steer to avoid you).

If you have the least doubt about being able to emerge safely (with due regard for other road users), stop and wait for a safe gap.

Make sure your vehicle is positioned correctly before and after a turn.

Turning left - Normal driving position, if the road is curved follow it round at a constant (1m.yd) distance.

Turning right - Just left of centre of road. If the road is narrow, or has been narrowed by parked vehicles/obstructions then keep well to the left.

When emerging to turn right drive the vehicle to the crown (middle of the road). When the front of your vehicle

is level with the middle of the road start to turn, making a neat 90 degree (right-angle) turn. Turning earlier would put you on the wrong side of the road and reduce your visibility.

When in your new road straighten the vehicle, resume your normal driving position, and check your mirrors (assess the following traffic).

10.9 Emerging - turning left

Side road into main road (minor into major)

The sequence to use for this would be as follows:

As soon as you see the junction, check your mirrors and assess the junction to get as much advance information as possible:

* What sort of junction is it? (Stop, give way, controlled, etc.)

* How many roads are joining?

* Any other road users about? (Are there vehicles waiting to emerge, pedestrians crossing, etc.)

* Width of road? (Remember that parked vehicles and obstructions will narrow the road.)

* Traffic conditions? (How busy is the road you are going to join - the frequency of vehicles crossing will tell you this.)

71

* Traffic signs?
(Will you have to stop or give way.)

Also, you should be assessing the junction for any restrictions to your view as you approach.

Ask yourself the following question:

"As I get closer to the junction, can I get a clear view of traffic approaching from the right and/or left?"

(Hedges, fences, walls, houses, parked vehicles - all of these could restrict your view.)

Use the MSPSL routine on approach:

MIRRORS:
Check for following traffic.

SIGNAL:
Indicate left.

POSITION:
Your normal driving position - do not veer in (you could hit or clip the kerb) or out but maintain a constant distance from the kerb. If, at the junction, the kerb curves round to the left, follow the curve and maintain a constant (1m/yd where possible) distance from it; this will then put you in the safest position for moving into the new road.

If, at the junction, the kerb is 'square', at 90°, do not steer left until just before the vehicle stops. Turning too early could cause you to drive over the kerb (very dangerous to pedestrians!)

SPEED:
As you approach the junction reduce your speed with the footbrake - it is the most effective method of slowing the vehicle down. It is not necessary to change down through the gears 4-3-2-1 on approach to a junction. It is much safer (both hands are kept on the wheel) and more economical; unnecessary gear changing wastes petrol and causes wear to the gearbox and transmission.

Do not coast (clutch held down) on approach. The gear you select will depend on road and traffic conditions and also your view on approach to, and at, the junction.

Generally speaking, however, at most junctions in urban areas your view will be restricted and you will usually have to virtually come to a stop in order to look properly. Obviously you would then select first gear.

First gear should be selected about a car's length from the junction; with the clutch coming to biting point about half a car's length from the junction. Your right foot should then be prepared to move from the accelerator to brake or vice versa , depending on your view at that time, and whether you decide to emerge or wait. Where possible, try and keep the car moving even if it is very slowly - this is because it is easier to move away if the car already has some forward movement.

Remember: at junctions your speed should be slow enough to enable you to look and take effective observation.

If, due to traffic conditions, you are unable to emerge and have to wait, apply the handbrake if you are going to be stopped for more than a moment. A moment here is defined as the time it would take to apply and release the handbrake without causing unnecessary delay.

The reason that the handbrake needs to be applied is to prevent your car, in the event of a rear end collision, from being 'shunted' out into approaching traffic.

LOOK:
When you can see clearly, take effective observation by looking right, left, then right again. Remember that the immediate danger is traffic coming from the right, so check to the right at the earliest opportunity. This will usually be before you actually get to the junction.

Check to the left for parked vehicles, pedestrians crossing or about to cross and also overtaking traffic which could be on your side of the road.

Check to the right again and if safe, i.e. if you can fit in with the traffic flow without causing other road users to change speed or direction, emerge and when in the new road and straight, check your mirror to assess the situation behind and, if safe, accelerate briskly and smoothly.

10.10 Emerging - turning right

Side road into main road (minor into major)

The sequence to use for this would be as follows:

As soon as you see the junction, check your mirrors and assess the junction to get as much advance information as possible:

*   What sort of junction is it?
    (Stop, give way, controlled, etc.)

*   How many roads are joining?

*   Any other road users about?
    (Are there vehicles waiting to emerge, pedestrians crossing, etc.)

*   Width of road?
    (Remember that parked vehicles and obstructions will narrow the road.)

*   Traffic conditions?
    (How busy is the road you are going to join - the frequency of vehicles crossing will tell you this.)

*   Traffic signs?
    (Will you have to stop or give way.)

Also, you should be assessing the junction for any restrictions to your view as you approach.

Ask yourself the following question:

"As I get closer to the junction, can I get a clear view of traffic approaching from the right and/or left?"

(Hedges, fences, walls, houses, parked vehicles - all of these could restrict your view.)

Use the MSPSL routine on approach:

MIRRORS:
Check for following traffic.

SIGNAL:
Indicate right.

POSITION:
Normally just left of the centre of the road. However, if the road is narrow or has been narrowed by parked vehicles you should keep well to the left.

SPEED:
As you approach the junction reduce your speed with the footbrake - it is the most effective method of slowing the vehicle down. It is not necessary to change down through the gears 4-3-2-1 on approach to a junction. It is much safer (both hands are kept on the wheel) and more economical; unnecessary gear changing wastes petrol and causes wear to the gearbox and transmission.

Do not coast (clutch held down) on approach. The gear you select will depend on road and traffic conditions and also your view on approach to, and at, the junction.

If on approach you can see clearly both ways (right/left/right) and it is safe to emerge you could possibly select 2nd gear.

Generally speaking, however, at most junctions in urban areas your view will be restricted and you will usually have to virtually come to a stop in order to look properly. Obviously you would then select first gear.

First gear should be selected about a car's length from the junction; with the clutch coming to biting point about half the car's length from the junction. Your right foot should then be prepared to move from the accelerator to brake or vice versa, depending on your view at that time, and whether you decide to emerge or wait. Where possible, try and keep the car moving even if it is very slow - this is because it is easier to move away if the car already has some forward movement.

Remember: at junctions your speed should be slow enough to enable you to look and take effective observation.

If, due to traffic conditions you are unable to emerge and have to wait, apply the handbrake if you are going to be stopped for more than a moment. A moment here is defined as the time it would take to apply and release the handbrake without causing unnecessary delay.

The reason that the handbrake needs to be applied is to prevent your car, in the event of a rear end collision, from being 'shunted' out into approaching traffic.

LOOK:
When you are in a position to see clearly, take effective observation by looking right/left/right. Remember that the immediate danger is from the right so check that way at the earliest opportunity - this will usually be before

you actually get to the junction. When turning right from a side road into a main road you will be crossing the path of approaching traffic; you must not make them change speed or direction.

You will also have to fit in with traffic travelling in the direction you want to travel in.

Remember - it is your responsibility to fit in with the traffic flow without causing road users to change speed or direction. As a guideline make sure that your car is in the new road, straight and parallel to the kerb before any oncoming traffic passes you. If you were not straight or parallel to the kerb you could cause other road users to swerve or brake to avoid you.

When in your new road, resume your normal driving position, check mirrors and, if safe, accelerate briskly and smoothly.

10.11 Emerging at a busy junction

Whilst waiting to emerge at a busy junction, you should be prepared to move off as soon as a safe gap appears. This will mean selecting 1st gear and preparing the car **before** the gap appears. Any delay when moving off could be vital, especially at a busy junction.

If traffic on the major road is so heavy that it becomes obvious that it will not be clear both ways, it is acceptable to emerge 'half-way' when it is clear from the right. Perhaps a Zebra/ Pelican crossing or Traffic Lights will slow or stop the flow sufficiently for you to emerge; drive the vehicle slowly towards the middle of the road, checking both ways; wait until a gap appears on the left, or a driver indicates for you to join the traffic flow; eye contact helps here.

10.12 SUMMARY: Dealing with junctions

* Get as much advance information as possible.

* What type of junction?

* Use of: Mirrors

Signal

Position

Speed

Look

11

DEALING WITH CROSSROADS (INCLUDING ROUNDABOUTS)

11.1 What is a crossroad?

A crossroad is where one road crosses another.

This could be:

* A major road crossing a minor road

* A minor road crossing a major road

* Controlled (traffic lights) crossroads

* Roundabouts

Whichever type of crossroad it is you would use the same sequence of approach: mirror/signal/position/speed/look.

Each type of crossroad is detailed as follows:

11.2 Major road crossing minor road

By anticipating and reading the road ahead you will be aware of approaching crossroads.

There are various 'clues' which will alert you to the approaching hazard (crossroads):

* Crossroads warning sign

* Gaps in rows of parked vehicles

* Gaps in rows of buildings/houses

* Hazard warning lines on approach to, and through, the crossroads. (Longer white lines in the middle of the road.)

* Road users emerging from, or entering, the crossroads.

If you are on a major road approaching a crossroad the sequence would be as follows:

CHECK MIRRORS

ASSESS CROSSROADS

CHECK MIRROR AGAIN

SLOW DOWN (Off gas, or brake and change down depending on how busy the junction is)

CHECK INTO MINOR ROADS (Be aware that although you are on the major road and have priority, vehicles could emerge without taking proper observation.

WHEN CLEAR of the crossroad check your mirror, if safe more gas to resume making normal progress.

11.3 Minor road crossing major road

If you are on a minor road approaching a crossroad and intending to follow the road ahead the sequence to use on approach would be:

Mirror: Assess situation behind

Signal: No signal necessary

Position: Normal driving position (3ft/1m from kerb)

Speed: Reduce speed with your brakes as necessary, do not rush up to junction. Select the appropriate gear depending on road and traffic conditions and your view on approach..

Look:
Right   ) Minimum once but as
Left   ) many times as is
Road ahead) necessary for the
Right   ) conditions.

As you cross the major road check right and left and as soon as you enter your new road check the mirror and if safe more gas and make normal progress.

When arriving at the crossroads and a vehicle approaching from the opposite direction arrives at his side of the junction at the same time, the priority is equal; 50/50.

However, be prepared either to give precedence, if the other vehicle moves first, or to move off: be positive in this situation.

Do **not** beckon the other driver or you could wave him into danger. If the other driver signals to you to move out it is up to you to make absolutely sure it is safe to emerge.

Make eye contact - look the driver in the eye and let him know that you have seen him.

When following the road ahead at crossroads (minor road crossing major) you will be crossing two lanes of traffic. You must do this without causing other road users to change speed or direction.

As a guideline, the back of your car must be **completely** in your new road before any traffic passes by. If you are not completely in the new road it could cause other road users to brake or swerve to avoid you.

11.4 Unmarked crossroads

Although there are relatively few unmarked crossroads you must still know how to deal with them.

Assume that all roads have equal priority, proceed with caution and be prepared to give way to other traffic. Consider that they may think they have 'right of way' and will carry on regardless.

If one road is wider or busier than the others it is often treated as having priority. However, never assume this to be the case and take the utmost care when emerging, crossing, or travelling through unmarked crossroads.

Use the mirror/signal/position/speed/look routine.

11.5 Controlled (traffic light) crossroads

Traffic lights are used to control the flow of traffic at crossroads which might otherwise become congested.

The traffic light sequence is as follows:

Colour	Meaning
Red	*Stop*
Red with Amber	*Stop*
Green	*Go* (only if the junction is clear)
Steady Amber	*Stop* (unless you have already crossed the white stop line or you are so close that to pull up would cause an accident)
Red	*Stop*

If the traffic lights have failed, proceed with the utmost caution - all roads have equal priority.

On approach to traffic lights use the mirror/signal/position/speed/look routine.

Anticipate, and prepare for, traffic light changes - plan your drive ahead.

When stopping at a red light, make sure you can see the traffic lights nearest to you. This will generally mean stopping about 1yd/1m before the white stop line. Although there is generally another traffic light opposite you, your view of this could be blocked by a large vehicle waiting to turn.

Whilst waiting at red traffic lights, **check all mirrors.** Door mirrors will let you know if there are cyclists/motorcyclists driving up along either side of your vehicle (especially important if you are turning left).

Look for clues to tell you when the lights are going to change:

*   Opposing set of lights sometimes visible

*   Opposing traffic flow stops

*   Pedestrian lights on red

You could also check your gauges, i.e. fuel, temperature, etc., while you are waiting.

Take the opportunity to look well ahead into the road you are going into - any obstructions which will cause you to change speed or direction.

Plan your drive and read the road ahead.

TURNING RIGHT
OFFSIDE - TO - OFFSIDE

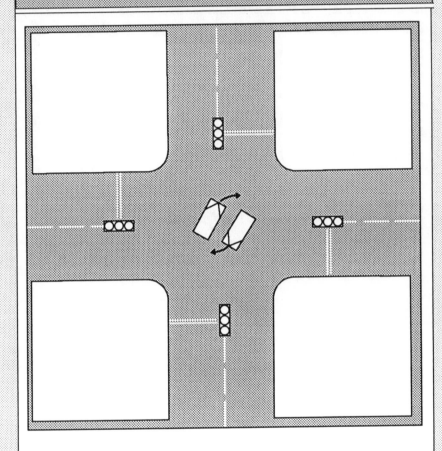

- The offside of the car is the drivers side.

- Pass behind any vehicle also turning right.

- Do not cross in front of traffic closely aproaching.

TURNING RIGHT
NEARSIDE - TO - NEARSIDE

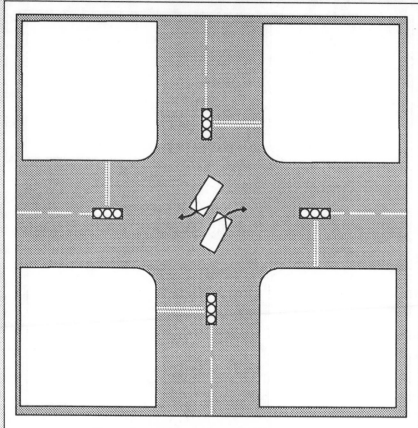

- The nearside of the car is the passenger side.

  You should turn nearside - to - nearside when:

- Road markings indicate.

- The layout of the junction makes it more practical.

- Other vehicles are incorrectly positioned.

In this situation your view will be restricted, so take particular care

11.6 Turning right at crossroads/ traffic lights

This can be done in two ways:

i) Turning offside-to-offside;

ii) Turning nearside-to-nearside.

Offside :
The side of the vehicle away from the kerb (the right-hand side, from your viewpoint in the driving seat).

Nearside :
The side of the vehicle which is normally near the kerb (the left-hand side, from your viewpoint in the driving seat).

11.7 Offside-to-offside

If you are on the major road at a crossroad (traffic light controlled, or otherwise) and intend to turn right and there is an oncoming vehicle wanting to turn to his right, the correct way to pass is to go offside-to-offside. This means passing behind the other vehicle, keeping it to your right. This method gives both drivers an unobstructed view of oncoming traffic.

Generally the rule is to turn offside-to-offside unless -

* Road markings indicate otherwise (painted white arrows on road).

* The layout of the junction makes it impractical (i.e. a staggered junction).

* Other traffic is incorrectly positioned.

11.8 Nearside-to-nearside

This means passing the other vehicle, keeping it on your left.

However, this reduces your view of oncoming traffic so take extra care - you need to be positioned so that you can see oncoming traffic but without getting in their way.

Local knowledge will come in very useful here - get to know the various crossroads in your area and whether they are offside-to-offside or nearside-to-nearside. In an area that you are unfamiliar with you should try to get as much advance information about the junction as you can. Even before you see the road markings you can watch how traffic positions itself and plan your manoeuvre accordingly.

11.9 Other traffic also turning right

At a traffic light crossroads, if you are intending to turn right and there is already a vehicle waiting to make the same turn as you, you must assess whether there is sufficient room for you to wait in the middle of the junction without obstructing any oncoming traffic which might be turning right. Even if there is no traffic about, leave a gap in case a vehicle does want to turn.

If there is insufficient space, wait behind the white stop line until you can safely move into position (as long as the traffic lights remain green).

You will need to assess the junction as you approach and decide if there is sufficient room to wait. Plan ahead and watch what the other traffic does: how many cars are waiting? etc. etc.

11.10 Yellow box junctions

Yellow box junctions may be found at certain busy junctions and crossroads. Their purpose is to keep junctions and crossroads clear, even at peak times. This ensures that traffic does not become grid-locked (one stationary lane of traffic blocking the flow of another lane of traffic, causing all traffic to be brought to a stop).

The rules for a yellow box junction are:

*   Do not enter unless your exit is clear.

*   You may enter and wait if you are turning right and are prevented from doing so only by oncoming traffic.

11.11 Roundabouts

Roundabouts are designed to keep traffic moving freely with the minimum of hold-ups or congestion.

On approach use the mirror/signal/position/speed/look routine.

Traffic circulates around a roundabout in a clockwise direction. You must give way to traffic from your immediate right. If the roundabout is clear, keep moving. Generally you will be able to get a good view on approach to a roundabout and this will enable you to plan your approach to, and through, the roundabout.

Stay in lane as you drive round the roundabout and signal left at the exit before the one by which you intend to leave. A quick glance over your left shoulder will tell you if there is any traffic coming up on your nearside.

At roundabouts be aware of the course taken by long vehicles and also cyclists/motorcyclists who could cut across in front of you.

11.12 Signals at roundabouts

There is a common belief among 'experienced' drivers that you should indicate only when leaving a roundabout. This is not true and is confusing and dangerous for other road users who do not know that driver's intentions.

Remember that signals help and warn other road users and when properly used will help to maintain the flow of traffic.

The following signals should be given for the following directions:

* "At the roundabout take the road off to the left, which is the first exit."

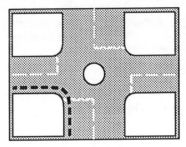

You should signal left on approach and as you turn.

* "At the roundabout follow the road ahead, which is the 2nd exit."

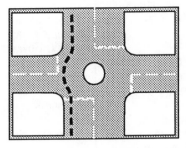

No signal on approach, then signal left at the exit before the one you want.

* "At the roundabout take the road off to the right, which is the third exit."

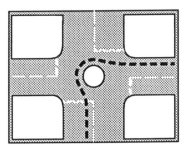

Signal right on approach and then signal left at the exit before the one you want.

Remember: Stay in lane and give signals correctly and properly timed.

11.13 Which lane?

There is a very simple guideline to use for roundabouts.

Imagine the roundabout is a clock face.

If you are leaving by an exit which is at '12 o'clock' or before, use the left-hand lane.

If you are leaving by an exit which is after '12 o'clock', use the right-hand lane on approach.

However, where there are directional arrows painted on the road, follow those.

If a roundabout has more than two lanes on approach use the lane most convenient for your exit.

When you have selected your lane, stay in it on approach and as you drive round the roundabout. Generally, roundabouts do not have lane markings, so you will have to imagine the road divided into lanes.

The most important points to remember about roundabouts are:

* Stay in lane

* Signal correctly

11.14 Mini-roundabouts

Mini-roundabouts are being used more and more at busy junctions to ease congestion and keep traffic moving.

Obviously because these junctions were not planned as roundabout sites, space is limited and hence the 'mini-roundabout'.

These are generally either:

* A raised circular hump.

* A white painted disc.

There may also be large white arrows painted on the road in a clockwise direction. Traffic flows in the same way and the same rules apply as to a standard roundabout.

Where there is a painted disc or circular hump try to avoid driving over it. However, in some situations this may be unavoidable; consider the following points:

* Length of your vehicle.

* Turning circle of your vehicle.

* Space available.

Where possible fit in with local practice and avoid causing obstruction or inconvenience to other road users.

If a mini-roundabout has approach roads which are all the same distance from each other and vehicles arrive at the roundabout at the same time, who gives way?

In the above situation, applying the rule of giving way to traffic on your immediate right would bring the traffic flow to a complete stop - each vehicle would have traffic on their immediate right! Be positive and be ready to make the first move - traffic on the roundabout has precedence.

11.15 SUMMARY: Crossroads

* Use the mirror/signal/position/speed/look routine.

* Regulate speed correctly on approach.

* Do not coast (clutch held down) on approach.

* Take effective observation before emerging.

* Emerge with due regard for approaching traffic.

* Position the vehicle correctly before and after turning right and left.

12

MEETING APPROACHING TRAFFIC SAFELY, ALLOWING ADEQUATE CLEARANCE

12.1 When does this happen?

In roads with parked vehicles each side the available width of road is narrowed considerably. Also if the road itself is physically narrow you will need to meet approaching traffic and allow them adequate clearance.

There are several situations which could arise:

* Parked vehicles each side with gaps.

* Parked vehicles each side with no gaps.

* Narrow road (no parked vehicles) with room for only one lane of traffic.

* Vehicle or obstruction (roadworks, etc.) causing the width of road to be narrowed.

Each of these will be dealt with in detail.

12.2 What to do . . .

In any road that is narrowed, remember the following points:

* Look further ahead, anticipate and plan your drive.
  Look for any gaps on both sides.

* Check your mirrors, slow down and be prepared to stop when meeting oncoming traffic.

* Never assume other road users will stop or give way to you. Always put yourself in a safe position.

* The closer you go to parked vehicles, the slower you must go.

* When driving through narrow gaps keep the vehicle straight. If the front goes through the back will go through!

Quite often, in a situation like this, other vehicles will 'flash' their headlamps at you. If they do this make sure:

* They have stopped or slowed right down (sometimes people 'flash' to say "I'm coming through", regardless!)

* Make sure the gap they have left you is safe to go through. (Do not assume, just because they have 'flashed', that you can get through. It is up to you to make sure it is safe to go through. Bear in mind that the driver who has flashed does not know the width of your vehicle or how much space he has allowed you. You must assess the situation and decide before committing yourself.)

MEETING APPROACHING TRAFFIC

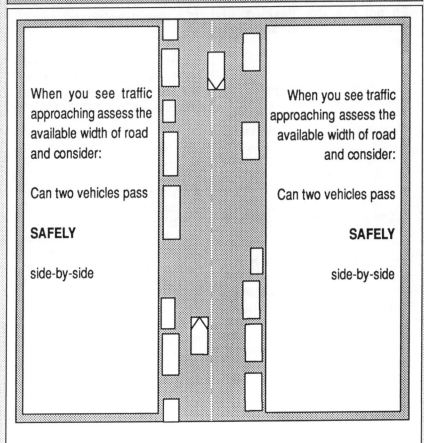

When you see traffic approaching assess the available width of road and consider:

Can two vehicles pass

SAFELY

side-by-side

When you see traffic approaching assess the available width of road and consider:

Can two vehicles pass

SAFELY

side-by-side

SAFETY FACTORS

- Check mirror, slow down, be prepared to stop.
  Always put yourself in a safe position.

- Look much further ahead, look for gaps, plan your drive.

- The closer you go to parked vehicles, the slower you go.

* If someone has 'flashed' and let you through, acknowledge this courtesy with a nod of the head and a smile. Do not take your hand off the wheel to wave, as this lessens your control of the vehicle.

Do not use the 'flashing' of headlamps in this situation yourself.

12.3 Parked vehicles (gaps)

When you enter a road that is narrow, or the road you are in narrows due to parked vehicles on either side, and you see oncoming traffic you must first assess the situation and ask yourself:

* "Can two vehicles pass safely side by side?"

If not, you must look for a convenient gap on your side of the road which you can pull into and let oncoming traffic pass. When you pull into a gap do not pull over too far (following traffic may think you are parking). As a guideline you should generally pull over about half the width of your vehicle. Do not stop too close to the parked vehicle behind which you are pulling up; you need enough space to be able to move away easily.

As a guideline when you stop, make sure you can see the back wheel(s) of the parked vehicle, and some of the road. This gap will give you sufficient room to manoeuvre around the parked vehicle.

If there is no convenient gap on your side look for a gap on the other side and wait opposite it; oncoming traffic can then pull into that gap to let you continue.

12.4 Parked vehicles (no gaps)

When you enter a road that is narrow or the road you are in narrows due to parked vehicles on either side, and you see oncoming traffic you must first assess the situation and ask yourself:

"Can two vehicles pass safely side by side?"

If the road you are in has parked vehicles each side with no gaps, you would then look for the narrowest vehicle to stop alongside (motorcycle, Mini, etc.) Remember, the closer you go to parked vehicles, the slower you must go. If there is no way that two vehicles could pass side by side, either you or the oncoming vehicle will have to reverse.

So, who should reverse? Bear in mind that priority is equal 50/50. Commonsense will normally dictate who should reverse, but take the following points into consideration:

* Who would find it easier and more convenient to reverse?

You would reverse if:

i) The other vehicle had a line of traffic behind him.

ii) The other vehicle is a large vehicle (bus, lorry, etc.) whose rear view is limited and for whom it is difficult to reverse.

iii) You had a space nearer to you than the other vehicle.

iv) The other vehicle was coming downhill. It is easier for you to reverse downhill than for the other vehicle to reverse uphill.

However, use your commonsense and do not assume that other road users will know any of the above or abide by it!

If the other driver 'flashes' you in the above situation, it will usually mean that he is prepared to reverse. However, do not assume this to be the case and wait to see what, if anything, he does. If he does reverse to a suitable passing place, make sure it is safe for you to go through the gap - when driving through a narrow gap make sure that your vehicle is straight; if the front goes through, the back will go through!

If someone has 'flashed' to let you through, acknowledge their courtesy with a nod of your head and a smile. Do not take your hand off the wheel to wave; this lessens your control of the vehicle.

Do not use the flashing of headlamps in this situation yourself.

12.5 Narrow roads

This situation can occur in rural areas where the road is wide enough for only one lane of traffic.

There could be passing places which may be signposted. They look like lay-bys but are there to enable traffic to pass safely side by side. If there are no 'proper' passing places you may have to use grass verges (beware of ditches!), entrances to fields, etc., to pull over onto, to allow sufficient clearance to oncoming vehicles.

On such roads consider the situation and circumstances and if you see approaching vehicles, note the location of the nearest passing place and decide whether to stop and reverse or wait opposite a passing place on the other side.

If the other driver 'flashes' you in the above situation, it will usually mean that he is prepared to reverse. However, do not assume this is to be the case and wait to see what, if anything, he does. If he does reverse to a suitable passing place, make sure it is safe for you to go through the gap - when driving through a narrow gap make sure that your vehicle is straight; if the front goes through, the back will go through!

If someone has 'flashed' to let you through, acknowledge their courtesy with a nod of your head and a smile. Do not take your hand off the wheel to wave; this lessens your control of the vehicle.

Do not use the flashing of headlamps in this situation yourself.

12.6 Vehicle or obstruction narrowing road

This situation will occur when there is just one vehicle (car, bus, delivery lorry, etc. etc.) or obstruction (roadworks, skip, fallen tree, etc.) on either your side of the road or the other.

The first thing to consider is that any vehicle or obstruction will narrow the available width of road - creating a 'new' width of road.

By 'reading' the road ahead you will be aware of parked vehicles/ obstructions and will be able to plan your drive around them.

Remember, the earlier that you see a 'hazard' (anything which contains an element of actual or potential danger) the more time it gives you to assess and decide what to do.

12.7 Obstruction/parked vehicle on your side of the road

If the obstruction is on your side of the road it is your responsibility to decide whether to go on or wait.

If you decide to go on you must be able to do so without causing oncoming vehicles to slow down or swerve to avoid you.

On a downhill gradient begin your braking in good time. Let traffic, especially heavy vehicles (buses, lorries, etc.) going uphill have a clear run. You can start off again downhill more easily than they can uphill.

The sequence to use on approach is:

MIRRORS:
Check following traffic.

POSITION:
Position your vehicle so that you have a good view of the road ahead - this will mean gradually moving to the right. However, consider oncoming traffic. Having looked and decided you then consider:

SPEED:
Select the most appropriate gear to take you past the obstruction briskly and safely or, if you are going to stop, reduce your speed with your brakes, stopping in a position which gives a clear view of the road ahead.

LOOK:
Assess the whole situation; to the front, rear and sides.

MIRRORS:

SIGNAL:
If necessary.

MANOEUVRE:
Drive past the obstruction briskly, check mirrors and resume normal driving position making normal progress.

HOW PARKED VEHICLES AFFECT THE ROAD WIDTH

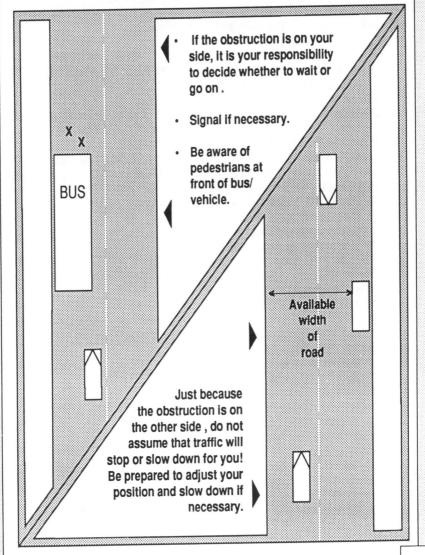

- If the obstruction is on your side, it is your responsibility to decide whether to wait or go on.

- Signal if necessary.

- Be aware of pedestrians at front of bus/vehicle.

BUS

Available width of road

Just because the obstruction is on the other side , do not assume that traffic will stop or slow down for you! Be prepared to adjust your position and slow down if necessary.

12.8 Obstruction/parked vehicle on other side of road

If the obstruction is on the other side of the road do not assume that you have priority.

The sequence should be:

* Check your mirrors, slow down and be prepared to stop.

* Adjust your position.
(Remember that an obstruction will narrow the width of the road, creating a new road width.)

Never assume that other road users will give way to you. Do not have an attitude of "it's my right of way, he should give way". Theoretically you may be right, but realistically you could end up **DEAD** right, which will not do you much good!
Your attitude should be "I'll adjust my position to take into account the fact that the oncoming vehicle will probably move out to pass the obstruction on his side."

By reading the road ahead and anticipating what other drivers are likely to do it will give you time to plan and decide what action to take.

On a downhill gradient begin your braking in good time. Let traffic, especially heavy vehicles (buses, lorries, etc.) going uphill have a clear run. You can start off again downhill more easily than they can uphill.

12.9 SUMMARY: meeting approaching traffic safely

* Use the mirror/signal/manoeuvre sequence.

* Allow adequate clearance when meeting traffic.

REMEMBER:

CHECK YOUR MIRRORS, SLOW DOWN AND BE PREPARED TO STOP.

NEVER ASSUME THAT ANYONE WILL GIVE WAY TO YOU.

NEVER ASSUME THAT YOU HAVE "RIGHT OF WAY".

13

CROSSING THE PATH OF OTHER VEHICLES SAFELY, ALLOWING ADEQUATE CLEARANCE

13.1 When does this happen?

You will cross the path of other vehicles in the following situations:

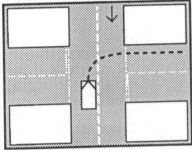

* Turning right from a major road into a minor road
* As above at crossroads

In the above situations you will be crossing the path of traffic approaching from the opposite direction.

This is a potentially dangerous situation. 75% of all accidents happen at junctions: twice as many accidents happen *leaving* a main road, as *entering* a main road.

13.2 You've been a pedestrian ...

When considering whether to drive across, ask yourself: "Could I walk across safely?" If the answer is "YES", then you could drive across!

Use your experience as a pedestrian to judge the speed of approaching traffic. Consider the speed of different types of vehicles; lorries, motorcycles, buses etc. etc.

Remember also, that at night it is more difficult to judge speed because the brain has so little information (only the size and number of headlamps) to work on.

When crossing the path of other vehicles:

* **Do not make other road users change their speed or direction**

This means they must not be made to brake or swerve to avoid you - this could obviously have disastrous consequences.

13.3 If in doubt ...

If you have the least doubt about being able to go safely in front of traffic closely approaching, then stop and wait.

If you are crossing more than one lane of traffic, be aware that traffic may be travelling at different speeds and very careful assessment must be made before driving across.

Always check your offside (driver's) door mirror before turning. This is to check that no vehicles are overtaking you (motorcyclists especially). This is particularly important if you have had to stop and wait.

As a guideline, when turning right from a major road into a minor road, you should have completed your turn and be in your normal driving position with the back of your car completely in the new road by the time any traffic goes by on the major road. This will ensure that you have allowed adequate clearance.

13.4 When to turn

You should start to turn when the front of your car is level with the middle of the road you are turning into. If you have to wait (because of approaching traffic) stop so that the front of your car is about 3ft/1m before the middle of the road. This is so that the vehicle is moving when you start turning.

Do not 'cut the corner' when you turn right. This restricts your field of vision and puts you on the wrong side of the road.

Make a neat 90° turn, imagine that there is a concrete bollard to help you avoid cutting the corner!

When you are waiting to turn right, try to keep your wheels straight. If you are 'shunted' from behind you will be pushed forward, but still be on your side of the road.

However, if your wheels are turned and you get 'shunted' from behind, you will be pushed into the path of approaching traffic.

Turning too early will cause you to cut the corner.

Turning too late will cause you to go wide, possibly striking the kerb. Also, by going wide you could 'invite' following vehicles to overtake you, with possible dangerous consequences.

13.5 Give way to . . .

When turning right, you must give way to pedestrians who are crossing the road you want to turn into.

If you have to wait, wait in a position just left of the middle of the road: if you had already started to turn and then you found you had to give way to pedestrians, you could end up broadside-on to approaching traffic which could be very dangerous.

Anticipate the actions of pedestrians and remember to check **both** sides of the road. Never beckon or signal to pedestrians, make eye contact with them to let them know you have seen them, the decision to cross must be made by them.

13.6 He's flashed me . . .

If, when waiting (or approaching), to turn right, you are 'flashed' or signalled by another vehicle, **do not** assume it is safe to cross.

They may be flashing at someone else; flashing is interpreted by different people in different ways.

You must make sure of two things:

* That the other vehicle has slowed down or stopped

* It is safe to cross. Consider motor-cyclists, cyclists etc. Approachimg on the inside. **never** use flashing headlamps in this way; it can be extremely misleading.

13.7 Safety Zone

Some right turns have a protected safety zone for vehicles waiting to turn right. This is usually a zone within diagonal white stripes. (see also chapter 18.7 - diagonal white lines)

If waiting traffic has filled up the safety zone, it is permissible to wait in the diagonal stripes immediately behind existing traffic. It would be advisable in these circumstances to keep your right foot lightly pressed on the brake pedal to activate the brake lights. The reason for this is that traffic approaching from behind may not be expecting stationary vehicles. The brake lights giving extra warning could prevent a rear end shunt.

13.8 Parked vehicles

If parked vehicles on left narrow the road you are turning into, it may be necessary to cut the corner and drive on the 'wrong' side of the road. However, before doing this it is VITAL that you can see clearly into the road, and can safely enter that road, before committing yourself; i.e. before starting to turn.

Any traffic coming down the road you are turning into has priority - they are already in the road and cannot easily take avoiding action. Therefore it is **your responsibility** to make sure you can safely enter the new road.

13.9 Turning right (major to minor) at crossroads

See pages 79 and 80 for diagrams.

In this situation the guidelines as outlined in sub-headings 13.2 - 13.8, apply.

However, you must consider that when turning nearside-to nearside your view will be restricted so exercise special care in these circumstances.

13.10 SUMMARY:

Crossing the path of other vehicles safely

* Use your experience as a pedestrian to judge when it is safe to drive across.

* Do not make other road users change speed or direction

* Take particular care at night, and in adverse weather conditions.

14

PASSING/OVERTAKING OTHER VEHICLES SAFELY ALLOWING ADEQUATE CLEARANCE

14.1 Definitions: passing/overtaking

PASSING is when you approach and pass a **stationary vehicle or obstruction** on your side of the road.

OVERTAKING is when you come up to and move past a **vehicle** which is travelling in the **same direction** as you are.

14.2 Passing other vehicles safely

Generally this will not cause too many problems and will usually mean a slight change of position or speed to pass the vehicle or obstruction.

Allow **adequate clearance** when passing stationary vehicles. Generally allow 1m/1yd or a car door's width when passing. Obviously the amount of room will depend on road and traffic conditions.

Be aware of the dangers from parked vehicles:

* Occupants may open doors.

* Pedestrians (especially children) may walk out between vehicles.

* Vehicles could move off without signalling.

Watch out for clues from parked cars:

* Occupants in car.

* Front wheels moving.

* Driver looking around.

* Brake lights on.

Consider what each of the above could mean and what is likely to happen, i.e. driver opens door, etc.

Again, careful planning and reading the road ahead will enable you to deal effectively with the situation.

Bear in mind the following points:

If a vehicle (or obstruction; roadworks, skips, fallen tree, etc.) is on your side the responsibility for deciding whether to go on or wait is **yours.**

You should go on only if you can do without making oncoming vehicles slow down or stop, otherwise you must wait.

If you see an oncoming vehicle, check your mirrors and make sure you slow down enough to be able to stop if necessary before the oncoming vehicle approaches.

Let traffic going uphill (especially heavy vehicles) have a clear run. You can start off again downhill much more easily than they can uphill.

14.3 Overtaking a moving vehicle

This is the most dangerous manoeuvre that you can carry out as a driver.

Ask yourself first: "Is it necessary?"

The amount of time that you save by overtaking is very rarely, if ever, worth it.

Also consider if you are going to be turning off shortly and, if so, it would be pointless to overtake.

When overtaking you will be on a collision course with traffic coming the other way and approaching them at the **combined** speed of both vehicles. For example, if you are travelling at 40 m.p.h. and a vehicle coming towards you is travelling at 60 m.p.h., the closing speed is 100 m.p.h. or 150ft/50m per second.

So you will understand how important it is to pick your time and place to be sure that you can get back to your side of the road safely without getting in the way either of the vehicle you are overtaking or those vehicles coming towards you.

14.4 Normally on the right ... but ...

Overtaking is normally on the right, *but* you can overtake on the left in the following circumstances:

i) when the driver in front of you has signalled that he intends to turn right, and you can overtake on the left without impeding other road users (and without entering an operational bus lane while doing so);

ii) when you want to turn left at a junction;

iii) when vehicles on the right are moving slower than you are when traffic is moving slowly in queues;

iv) in one way streets that are *not dual carriageways* where vehicles may pass on either side.

14.5 Where not to overtake

Certain places are not suitable (as shown in the Highway Code) because:

* You cannot see the road ahead (bends, brow of hill, etc.)

* You must allow for the movement of other road users (pedestrian crossings, junctions, etc.)

* You do not have a first class zone of vision (parked vehicles/obstruction obscuring your view).

14.6 Points to consider

Before overtaking you must consider:

a) The speed of your vehicle;

b) The speed of the vehicle to be overtaken;

c) The speed limit in force (also consider the road and weather conditions).

Also, try and judge the speed of any vehicle coming towards you - think in ft/m per second to give you a better 'feel' for judging speed and distance.

The smaller the difference between your speed and the speed of the vehicle(s) you are overtaking, the more time and clear road you need.

Consider also that the speed of a large vehicle (bus, lorry) can vary a great deal. Because of the weight, such a vehicle would be slowed considerably by uphill gradients. However, when travelling downhill the same vehicle, assisted by gravity, could speed up considerably.

14.7 Routine for overtaking

1. POSITION:
   Make sure you have a good view.

2. SPEED:
   Enough in reserve to overtake the vehicle? Change down to a more responsive gear, if necessary.

3. LOOK:
   Assess the whole situation.

4. MIRRORS:
   Make sure it is safe.

5. SIGNAL:
   If necessary.

6. MANOEUVRE:
   Overtake as briskly as you can. When clear of the vehicle move back in.

When overtaking, allow sufficient clearance to the vehicle being overtaken - give cyclists at least 6ft/2m (they could swerve or wobble). **After** overtaking do not cut in, slow down or stop.

14.8 SUMMARY: passing/overtaking other vehicles safely

PASSING

* Consider available width of road.

* Allow adequate clearance to stationary vehicles.

* Be prepared to stop and let oncoming traffic go by.

OVERTAKING

* Is it necessary?

* Consider speeds of vehicles involved.

* Use PSL/MSM routine.

15

FOLLOWING BEHIND OTHER VEHICLES AT A SAFE DISTANCE

15.1 What is a safe distance?

When following behind other vehicles remember to allow the necessary stopping distance (see page 53). These stopping distances should be doubled in wet weather and quadrupled (4x) in icy conditions.

On the open road in good conditions you should leave a gap of 1yd/1m for each m.p.h. between yourself and the vehicle you are following, i.e. if you are travelling at 50 m.p.h. you should leave a gap of 50 metres.

However, in heavy traffic in a built-up area it is unrealistic and not possible to allow that distance.

A reasonable compromise is to drive allowing at least the braking distance (45ft at 30 mph) between yourself and the vehicle in front. Never leave a gap less than your thinking distance (30ft at 30mph) - this will reduce your safety margins too much. Remember that by allowing yourself room to stop you are giving yourself **time to react.**

A method of ensuring that you leave a safe distance is the 2 second rule which works in the following way:

15.2 The 2 second rule

When the vehicle in front of you passes a fixed point (lamp-post, bridge, etc.) count 1 second 2 seconds by saying it to yourself slowly. If you reach the same fixed point before you have finished saying 1 second, 2 seconds, then you are too close and should slow down to increase the gap.

Travelling at 50 mph you are covering 75 feet per second, therefore in 2 seconds you will have travelled 150 feet which is approximately the overall stopping distance.

At speeds below 40 mph the 2 second rule does not work because a 2 second gap would give unrealistically large spacing between vehicles - especially in a built-up area - and other road users would continually be moving into that space causing you to constantly slow down - which in turn can cause following traffic to become frustrated and angry.

THE TWO SECOND RULE

- By using the 2 second rule you will be able to allow sufficient clearance between your car and the vehicle in front.

- The 2 second rule relates to a distance of 1m / 1 yd. per m.p.h. i.e. at 60 mph you would leave 60 m / yds.

- The 2 second rule works at speeds of 40 m.p.h. and over. At speeds lower than that the gap would be unreasonably large.

When the vehicle in front passes a fixed point, count 1 second 2 seconds by saying it slowly. If you can say it before you reach the same fixed point, then you are following at a safe distance. If not, ease back to a safe distance.

NOTE:

The fixed point could be a lamp-post, telegraph pole, etc.,etc. On a motorway you could use a bridge or emergency phonebox as the fixed point.

15.3 Adequate clearance in traffic queues

When coming to a stop behind a queue of stationary traffic, always stop so that you can see the back wheels of the vehicle in front of you, and some of the road between the two vehicles.

This gap will be approximately 6ft/ 2m.

This is your safety gap and three reasons for leaving this gap are:

i) If you are on a gradient and the vehicle in front rolls back, you will have a safety margin which will give you time to warn him (horn signal).

ii) If the vehicle in front stalls, you will have sufficient room to drive around him.

iii) If you are the last vehicle in a traffic queue and you see in your mirror a vehicle coming up very fast, which may not have realised the traffic was stopped, you have a 'safety zone' into which to drive forward. By doing this you will lessen the extent of any damage due to a 'rear-end shunt'.

15.4 SUMMARY: following behind other vehicles at a safe distance

* Consider the overall stopping distance (adverse weather conditions).

* The 2 second rule.

* Stopping behind stationary traffic - leave a 'safety gap'.

16

DEALING WITH PEDESTRIAN CROSSINGS

16.1 Two types of pedestrian crossings

Uncontrolled : Zebra crossings

Controlled : Pelican crossings (light controlled)
School Patrol
Police/Traffic Warden

Each of these will be explained in detail:

16.2 Zebra crossings

Zebra crossings are uncontrolled (i.e. pedestrians cannot control the traffic). It is up to drivers to stop and allow pedestrians to cross.

This crossing gets its name because of the black and white stripes that form the crossing. A zebra crossing can also be identified by white zig-zag lines on approach (minimum of 2 max 18 - depending on space available) and flashing amber beacons on black and white striped poles. These beacons are known as 'Belisha' beacons, named after
Lord Hore-Belisha who was Minister of Transport in 1934 when they were introduced.

16.3 Within the zig-zag lines

On each side of the crossing (or on one side only in the case of one-way traffic) an area known as 'the controlled area' is marked by a pattern of lines consisting of:

i)   The give way line - a white broken line across the road 1 metre from the striped (black and white) area.

ii)   The zig-zag lines - two or more white broken lines extending along the carriageway in a zig-zag fashion away from the crossing, starting 150mm from the give way line and ending 150mm from the terminal line.

There should be not less than 8 (but this may be 2 where compliance is not practicable) and not more than 18 of the zig-zags.

iii) The terminal line - the end of each zig-zag line must be marked by a stop mark.

Slight departures from the specifications provided have no significance if the general indications are not materially impaired.

Within this controlled area there are certain things you must not do . . .

ZEBRA CROSSINGS

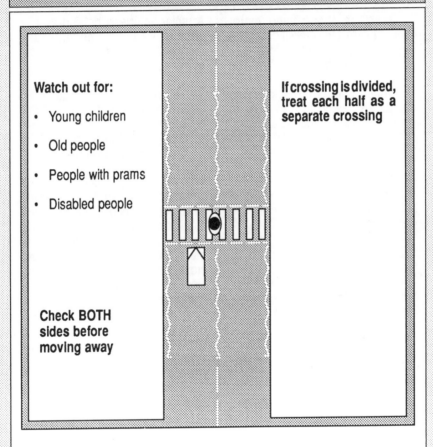

Watch out for:

- Young children
- Old people
- People with prams
- Disabled people

Check BOTH sides before moving away

If crossing is divided, treat each half as a separate crossing

SAFETY FACTORS

- Use MSM on approach.
  (Arm signal if you are first vehicle and have time).
- Correct speed on approach.
- Stop when necessary.
- Do not overtake on approach.
- Do not beckon to pedestrians.

16.4 No overtaking, no parking, no stopping

Within the zig-zag lines on approach to a zebra crossing a driver **MUST NOT:**

i) **Overtake** the moving motor vehicle nearest the crossing, or pass the leading vehicle* which has stopped to give way to a pedestrian.

ii) **Park** - this would obviously cause danger by restricting the view of pedestrians and other road users. Exceptions to this are pedal bicycles and mopeds (solo).

iii) **Stop** - stopping to let people in or out of the car is illegal and again would cause danger by blocking the view of other road users.

Exceptions to iii) Stopping are as follows:-

* If you are stopping to let people cross on the zebra.

* If you have to stop to avoid an accident or due to circumstances beyond your control.

* If you have to stop for any of the emergency services, building operations or essential services.

* If you are stopping to make a left or right turn.

* A bus (not on an excursion or tour) may stop (after **passing** the crossing) to allow people to get on or off the bus.

* Notes on overtaking.

Within the zig-zag lines on approach to a zebra crossing you must not overtake the moving **motor vehicle** nearest the crossing.

A motor vehicle is defined as any vehicle which is mechanically propelled. The source of mechanical power could be:

Petrol (cars, motorcycles, etc.)
Electricity (milk floats, etc.)
Oil (lorries, cars, etc.)
Gas (LPG adapted vehicles)
Steam (Steam rollers, etc.)

With the zig-zag lines on approach you must not pass the leading vehicle which has stopped. Note, however, that in a one-way street if a crossing has a central island or refuge, the parts on each side are separate crossings. If a vehicle stops on one side, you may pass ahead of that vehicle along the other side.

A vehicle is defined as any method of transport and originates from the latin **vehere** : to carry.
A vehicle, therefore, could be:

A cycle,
A ridden horse,
Horse drawn vehicle,
Street barrow,

as well as all forms of motor vehicles.

However, even if there are no zig-zag lines, never overtake just before a zebra crossing.

16.5 Approaching a zebra crossing

Check your mirrors, slow down (off the gas/brake and select lower gear; depending on prevailing circumstances), check both sides of the crossing.

In a busy high street you should be driving at a speed slow enough that you could stop safely if necessary.

The speed you approach at will depend on the following factors:

* How busy the road is (how much pedestrian traffic about).

* Weather conditions (if it is raining pedestrians could dash across a crossing, and also you need more room to stop: overall stopping distance is doubled in wet weather).

* Time of day (schools starting/ finishing).

Treat the zebra crossing as an extension of the pavement and give precedence to pedestrians. If a zebra crossing is divided by a central island each half forms a separate crossing.

16.6 Stopping when necessary

On approach to a zebra crossing you should use the mirror/signal/ manoeuvre routine as follows:
MIRROR:
Assess following traffic situation.

SIGNAL:
An arm signal (slow down/ stopping) will help and warn other road users:
  Pedestrians waiting at crossing
  Following traffic
  Oncoming traffic
Give an arm signal if you are the first to approach and you have the time. (Remember, you will have to open the window!)

Give the arm signal for as long as it takes to say "I am slowing down and stopping".

MANOEUVRE:
Gently brake to a stop at the give-way line (1m from striped area). If stopping for more than a moment apply the handbrake and prepare the car, ready to move away as soon as any pedestrians have cleared the crossing.

If a pedestrian has stepped onto the crossing you **must** stop. Even if the pedestrian is standing on the pavement with one foot on the crossing you must stop.

This also applies to people with prams, push-chairs, buggies, etc. If someone is standing on the pavement with their buggy on the crossing it has the same legal meaning as if someone had their foot on the crossing: drivers **must** stop.

If the pedestrians obviously want to cross you should stop. If they want to cross pedestrians will be waiting on the pavement by the zebra, or walking purposefully towards it.

When you have stopped to let people cross **do not beckon to them.** If they want to cross it is their decision.

them into danger (a motorcyclist or other road user might be approaching and might not be aware of the pedestrian).

When stopped it is recommended that you make eye contact with the pedestrians (look them in the eye) to let them know you have seen them.

It is a legal requirement to give precedence to pedestrians until they are out of danger; consider the type of pedestrian: children, old people etc..

During traffic hold-ups leave the zebra crossing clear.

16.7 Watch out for ...

At zebra crossings be especially aware of:

* Young children (may dash across road).

* Old people (may be standing back from the crossing).

* Blind people* (will usually have a white stick and a guide dog).

* People with prams/buggies, etc.

* Disabled/infirm people.

* A person who is blind as well as deaf may carry a white stick with two red reflectorised bands - these bands indicate that the person is deaf.

People wearing personal headphones may not hear your

vehicle approach - look for clues such as wires or tape player on belt.

16.8 SUMMARY: Zebra crossings

* Use the mirror/signal/manoeuvre routine on approach (consider arm signal).

* Approach at the proper speed.

* Stop when necessary.

* Do not overtake at or near a zebra crossing.

* Do not signal to pedestrians.

16.9 Pelican crossings

This is a controlled crossing: pedestrians operate traffic light signals by pushing a button to bring traffic to a stop at the crossing.

This crossing gets its name from the fact that it is a PEdestrian LIght CONtrolled crossing.

The pelican crossing has zig-zag lines on approach and traffic lights mounted on grey posts. The control button is in a yellow box on the post 1.5m from the ground.

Note: If a pelican crossing is under construction but not yet operating, it has no legal status as a crossing.

PELICAN CROSSINGS

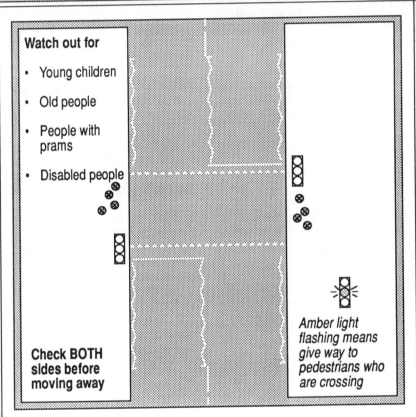

Watch out for

- Young children
- Old people
- People with prams
- Disabled people

Check BOTH sides before moving away

Amber light flashing means give way to pedestrians who are crossing

SAFETY FACTORS

- Use MSM on approach.
- Correct speed on approach.
- Stop when necessary.
- Do not overtake on approach.
- Do not beckon to pedestrians.

On approach check both sides of the crossing

(The exception to this would be where a pelican is replacing a zebra crossing. It would be treated as a zebra until the pelican crossing was operational).

If pelican crossing lights have failed, it becomes a zebra crossing and you must abide by the regulations governing such a crossing.

However, it must be stressed that other road users, especially pedestrians, could become confused and unsure in the above situation.

Proceed with extreme caution.

16.10 Within the zig-zag lines

On each side of the crossing (or on one side in the case of one-way traffic) an area known as 'the controlled area' is marked by a pattern of lines consisting of:

i)   The stop line - a solid white line across the road 1 metre from the area marked by studs: 'the crossing area'.

ii)   The zig-zag lines - two or more white broken lines extending along the carriageway in a zig-zag fashion away from the crossing, starting 150mm from the stop line and ending 150mm from the terminal line. There should be not less than 8 (but this may be 2 where compliance is not practicable) and not more than 18 of the zig-zags.

iii)   The terminal line - the end of each zig-zag line must be marked by a stop mark.

Slight departures from the specifications provided have no significance if the general indications are not materially impaired.

Within this controlled area there are certain things you must not do . . .

16.11 No overtaking, no parking, no stopping

Within the zig-zag lines on approach to a pelican crossing a driver **MUST NOT:**

i)   **Overtake** the moving motor vehicle nearest the crossing, or pass the leading vehicle* which has stopped to give way to a pedestrian.

ii)   **Park** - this would obviously cause danger by restricting the view of pedestrians and other road users. Exceptions to this are pedal bicycles and mopeds (solo).

iii)   **Stop** - stopping to let people in or out of the car is illegal and again would cause danger by blocking the view of other road users.

Exceptions to iii) Stopping are as follows:-

*   If you are stopping to let people cross on the pelican.

*   If you have to stop to avoid an accident or due to circumstances beyond your control.

*   If you have to stop for any of the emergency services, building operations or essential services.

* If you are stopping to make a left or right turn.

* A bus (not on an excursion or tour) may stop (after **passing** the crossing) to allow people to get on or off the bus.

* Notes on overtaking

Within the zig-zag lines on approach to a pelican crossing you must not overtake the moving **motor** vehicle nearest the crossing.

A motor vehicle is defined as any vehicle which is mechanically propelled. The source of mechanical power could be:

> **Petrol** (cars, motorcycles, etc.)
> **Electricity** (milk floats, etc.)
> **Oil** (lorries, cars, etc.)
> **Gas** (LPG adapted vehicles)
> **Steam** (steam rollers, etc.)

Within the zig-zag lines on approach you must not pass the leading vehicle which has stopped. Note, however, that in a one-way street if a crossing has a central island or refuge, the parts on each side are separate crossings. If a vehicle stops on one side, you may pass ahead of that vehicle along the other side.

A vehicle is defined as any method of transport and originates from the latin word **vehere** : to carry.
A vehicle, therefore, could be:

> A cycle,
> A ridden horse,
> Horse drawn vehicle,
> Street barrow,

as well as all forms of motor vehicles.

However, even if there are no zig-zag lines, never overtake just before a pelican crossing.

16.12 Pelican light sequence

Red . . . . .Stop.

Flashing Amber . Give way to pedestrians on the crossing.

Green . . . . Go (only if there are no pedestrians on the crossing).

Steady Amber . . . . . . Stop (unless you have already crossed the white stop line or are so close to it that to pull up would cause an accident).

Red . . . . Stop.

This sequence differs from that of 'ordinary' traffic lights in that red and amber do not show at the same time, and there is a flashing amber.

16.13 Stopping when necessary

On approach to a pelican crossing you should first check your mirrors and then assess the situation ahead, asking yourself the following questions:

* "What colour are the lights?"

* "Are there any pedestrians at or near the crossing?"

* "What might I expect to happen?"

* "How much do I adjust my speed?"

By reading the road ahead and anticipating pelican light changes you will have time to assess and decide the correct speed to approach and whether to stop or not.

Look for any pedestrians at or near the crossing. Assume that any pedestrians at the crossing have pushed the button. Expect the lights to change and be driving at a speed slow enough that you can stop safely, if necessary.

However, do not be driving so slowly that waiting pedestrians consider it an 'invitation' to cross. This could cause an extremely dangerous situation - other road users could become confused and pedestrians might start to cross when it was not safe.

Even if there are no pedestrians around do not assume the lights will remain as they are - someone may have pushed the button and then run off!

16.14 Divided pelican crossings

You may come across pelican crossings which have a dividing refuge or central reservation.

These types of crossings are either staggered or straight.

If the crossing is staggered, treat each half as a separate crossing.

However, if it is straight you must treat it as one crossing and you must wait for people crossing from the further side of the refuge or central reservation.

When you are stopped and waiting for pedestrians to cross, do not rev your engine or harass the pedestrians in any way.

An audible signal will sound when it is safe to cross for blind people. This signal only operates whilst the pelican lights are on red for drivers.

Give way to pedestrians who are still crossing when the light allows vehicles to move.

16.15 SUMMARY: Pelican crossings

* Use the mirror/signal/manoeuvre routine. Arm signal not necessary (pedestrians control traffic).

* Approach at the proper speed (anticipate light changes).

* Stop when necessary.

* Do not overtake at or near a pelican crossing.

* Do not signal to pedestrians.

16.16 Other controlled crossings

Other pedestrian crossings may be controlled by:

* **School Crossing Patrol (lollipop lady)**

* **Police Officer**

* **Traffic Warden**

School crossing patrol:

Usually known as 'lollipop-ladies' (because of the shape of their 'stop' sign) they will be controlling traffic near schools, where children will be wanting to cross the road. The children will be going to or from school, or on their way from one part of a school to another.

A school crossing patrol will usually be on duty between 8 a.m. and 5.30 p.m.

The patrol must wear the approved uniform and will carry a circular 'stop, children' sign on a pole. When this sign is shown, drivers must stop, and remain stopped whilst the sign is being shown. They must not continue until the sign is removed.

In places of particular danger, there may be flashing amber signals below the warning sign which tells you there is a patrol operating ahead. These flashing amber signals are activated by the 'lollipop' person as and when required.

Police Officer:

Obey all signs given by a police officer controlling the traffic. See the Highway Code for these signs.

Be prepared to give way to people who are still crossing when you get the signal to move. Police officers may act as school crossing patrols.

Traffic warden:

Obey all signs given by traffic warden controlling the traffic.

Be prepared to give way to people who are still crossing when you get the signal to move. Traffic wardens may act as school crossing patrols.

16.17 SUMMARY: Other controlled crossings

* Use mirror/signal/manoeuvre on approach.

* Approach at the proper speed.

* Comply with signals given to you.

* Do not drive on until it is safe to do so - give way to people who are still crossing when you get the signal to move.

17

ANTICIPATING THE ACTIONS OF PEDESTRIANS/CYCLISTS/OTHER DRIVERS

17.1 Anticipate - think for them : pedestrians

As a driver you must consider other more vulnerable road-users, such as:

Pedestrians, Especially:
>Young Children
>School Children
>People with Prams
>Old People
>The Handicapped

Young Children: do not have the same awareness of danger as adults. They also cannot judge speed and distance.

They are quite likely to do things suddenly on impulse, when their attention is distracted by things which they find more interesting; an ice-cream van, friends on the other side of the road or animals.

Whenever you see children on the pavement you must think for them and remember that they could dash into the road without warning.

School Children: get to know the school times in your area. At those times the traffic will increase due to parents driving to and from school, and waiting outside school to collect their children.

Remember that children are more interested in getting home than road safety, so take extra care. There will also be children on bikes, maybe riding up to 4 abreast (side-by-side). Give them plenty of room when passing and be ready in case they swerve or change direction suddenly.

Also, bear in mind that mums picking up children may have their attention distracted by occupants of the car, so be prepared for the unexpected!

People with Prams: be aware that at zebra crossings the pram or buggy might be put on the crossing before the person pushing it has stepped onto the crossing. In this situation you must stop. On country roads pedestrians with prams might be on your side of the road - keep your speed down!

Old People: elderly people do not move as quickly as younger people, and they find judging speed and distance more difficult as they get older.

Also, sight and hearing deteriorate with age; elderly pedestrians may not be able to see or hear approaching traffic clearly.

Allow them more time at pedestrian crossings and do not harass them by revving your engines or edging forward; this could worry and distress them.

When you are waiting in traffic queues watch out for pedestrians (especially the elderly and young children) crossing between cars. This may occur more frequently in wet weather with pedestrians taking the shortest route or dashing for cover.

The Handicapped: handicapped (disabled people) need more time when crossing the road, so be patient. Blind people usually carry a white stick and have a guide dog (usually a labrador or golden retriever). Blind and deaf people will carry a white stick with two red reflectorised bands.

17.2 Think for them: cyclists/motor cyclists

Where possible, allow cyclists a clearance of 2m/6ft.

Be aware that cyclists might wobble and swerve suddenly and without warning. This could be because of pot-holes, drain covers, etc.

If a cyclist is looking over his right shoulder it could be that he wants to turn right and he is checking for following traffic - make allowances for this and be prepared to 'hold back' to let him get into position.

Cyclists carrying bulky objects might weave along the road as their control and balance is affected.

All cyclists are affected by adverse weather conditions:

Rain:
In the rain cyclists will tend to keep their heads down to avoid rain coming straight into their faces. This obviously restricts their vision and they might not look where they are going. Smooth wet surfaces are very slippery and therefore extremely dangerous to cyclists - when braking, the front or back wheel could slide sideways out from underneath the rider. On such surfaces allow extra clearance to cyclists.

Cold Weather:
Cyclists hands will get very cold even with gloves on and this will mean that their physical reactions are slowed down; i.e. pulling on the brakes etc.

Stong Winds:
Cyclists are particularly affected by side-winds (blowing them off course, etc.) especially on open roads. Head-winds could cause a cyclist to keep his head down and stand up on the pedals to maintain headway. Both of these actions will result in a loss of vision and balance, so give the cyclists more room.

Always consider cyclists when parked and opening doors to get in or out.

Before turning left, always check your nearside mirror for cyclists who may be riding between your vehicle and the left-hand kerb.

Child cyclists are a particular hazard: They could be riding on the pavement one moment, then suddenly dart into the road. If they are riding in an unorthodox way; 'wheelies', 'two-up', etc. etc. take this as a warning to be extra careful, and be prepared to slow down or stop if necessary.

If you need to make cyclists aware of your presence, use one or two short 'taps' on the horn. A longer note may alarm or startle them (especially children).

It should be noted that some childrens bikes (of the B.M.X. variety) do not have brakes!

17.3 Anticipating other drivers

With experience you will learn to identify 'signals' or clues that are given by other drivers that can alert you to what they might be going to do.

The following observation links will help:

* **DRIVER TALKING TO PASSENGERS: Drivers attention is obviously distracted causing him to possibly indicate and brake late.**

* **DRIVER USING CAR-PHONE HAND-SET WHILST MOVING: Obviously the drivers control will be seriously affected. If he is holding the phone with one hand, how can he control the car (steer, change gear etc.) properly?**

He might even have the phone cradled on his shoulder using his head to keep it in place. How can

he then use his mirrors properly?

* **ONE OR MORE MIRRORS MISSING OR BROKEN: Driver will have limited rear vision (especially if the interior mirror is missing). Assume that he has no knowledge of the traffic situation behind and take particular care when passing such a vehicle.**

* **VEHICLE BRAKE LIGHTS GO ON FOR NO APPARENT REASON: Look for possible reasons; stopping to let passengers in or out, looking for a particular house or shop etc. etc.**

* **VEHICLE SLOWS DOWN FOR NO APPARENT REASON: If no brake lights are showing it could be that they do not work! Or possibly the driver is slowing down using the gears (this will not activate the brake lights, wastes petrol and is less safe).**

* **DELIVERY VEHICLES: May be stopping frequently, driver will be getting out of vehicle and then could open rear doors which might swing out, causing danger to other road-users. Obvious delivery collection vehicles are post-office vans/milk-floats/freight firms etc. etc.**

The above are just a few examples - you will encounter many others in your driving career. Learn from these experiences and use any knowledge gained to anticipate and deal with a similar thing happening again. Being prepared will help you to deal with hazards effectively and safely.

17.4 SUMMARY: Anticipating the actions of other road users

* Pedestrians/cyclists/motor cyclists: Think for them.

* Watch for clues as to what drivers/ riders may do.

* Make early use of available information and ask yourself:
What could happen?
What action should I take?

* Plan ahead and consider all possible hazards.

18

TRAFFIC SIGNS AND ROAD MARKINGS

18.1 Traffic signs and road markings

There are many traffic signs and road markings and it is important that they are understood. After all, they are there for a reason.

All signs and markings must be seen in good time so that the driver can take in the information, process it and decide what action to take.

Once the sign or marking has been seen the driver should look further ahead to assess the conditions/layout to which it refers.

18.2 Traffic signs ...

The system of signs used in the U.K. is international, so if you drive abroad you will understand the road signs even if you do not understand the language.

Traffic signs can be divided into 3 categories:

1) Circular signs giving orders.

2) Triangular signs giving warnings.

3) Rectangular signs giving information/directions

Wherever possible, symbols are used because they are more easily seen. However, there may be additional wording where necessary.

Different colours are used to subdivide the categories.

* Blue circles give a positive instruction.

* Red rings or circles give a negative instruction.

* Blue rectangles give general information.

* Green rectangles give directions on primary routes.

There are, however, some exceptions to the shape and colour rule. The octagonal stop sign is one such example. With such a distinctive shape its meaning can be recognised even if the stop line and face of the sign is obscured by snow.

For a full range of signs and their meanings, you should study 'The Highway Code', and 'KNOW YOUR TRAFFIC SIGNS'.

18.3 Road markings

Road markings also give information, either on their own or in conjunction with signs.

LINES ALONG THE ROAD

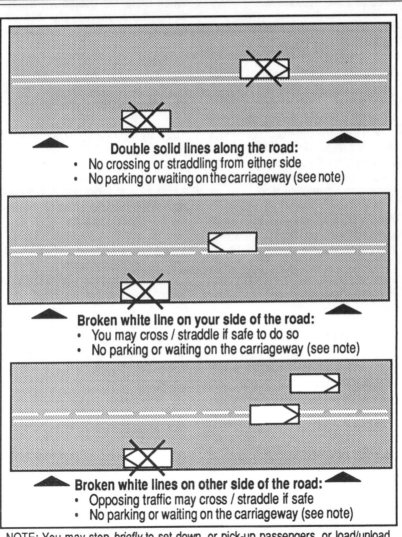

Double solid lines along the road:
- No crossing or straddling from either side
- No parking or waiting on the carriageway (see note)

Broken white line on your side of the road:
- You may cross / straddle if safe to do so
- No parking or waiting on the carriageway (see note)

Broken white lines on other side of the road:
- Opposing traffic may cross / straddle if safe
- No parking or waiting on the carriageway (see note)

NOTE: You may stop *briefly* to set down, or pick-up passengers, or load/unload goods. If a vehicle has stopped for the above reason, you may cross the solid line (when safe!) to pass it.

117

Road markings help lane discipline by guiding drivers as to where to position their vehicles.

As a general rule, the more white paint there is on the road, the more important the message is.

18.4 Give way lines

These are broken white lines across your half of the road.

If there is a double row you **must** give way to traffic on the major road. This does not necessarily mean that you have to stop; if you can see it to be clear you could emerge without coming to a complete stop.

If there are double broken lines within a roundabout, you **must** give way to traffic from your immediate right.

However, if there is a single broken line you should give way.

18.5 Stop lines

A stop line is a solid white line showing where you **must** stop. You will find such a line at stop signs, traffic lights, level crossings, swing bridges/ferries and police controlled junctions.

At junctions with stop lines, you **must** stop. The reason for this is so that you can take effective observations; these junctions will generally have restricted visibility due to bends, hills etc.

18.6 Lines along the road

Again, the general rule is the more white paint, the more important the message.

When there are double white lines along the road (usually, but not always, in the middle), you **must not**:

* Park or wait on the carriageway.

* Cross or straddle the solid line which is nearer to you.

You may stop *briefly* to set down or pick up passengers, or load/unload goods.

If both lines are continuous, traffic on both sides must not cross or straddle the line nearest to them.

If the line nearest to you is broken you may cross if it is safe to do so, and you can get back to your side of the road before there is another solid white line on your side. There may be large white arrows (pointing left) painted on the road as an advanced warning of the line becoming solid. Do not start to overtake if you see these arrows.

On some roads you might have sufficient space to overtake without crossing a solid line.

Where opposing streams of traffic need to be kept apart (for safety reasons) the gap between the lines is widened and the space in between is covered with white diagonal stripes. Do not enter this area, except in an emergency.

A single broken white line along the road is used as a centre line marking or lane marking.

When these lines become longer it is a warning of a hazard:

Bend
Junction
Brow of a hill

So, take note of any such warnings and assess the hazard as you approach.

If there is a solid white line along the edge of the road this is also a hazard warning. The hazard could be a sharp bend, hills, concealed entrances, etc. etc. Where the line is broken at the edge of the road this is used to mark the edge and make it more visible; this is especially helpful at night.

A thicker solid white line is used to mark the edge of a bus-lane.

18.7 Diagonal white stripes

These are used for the following reasons:

* To separate streams of traffic which may be dangerous to each other.

* To protect traffic turning right.

* To filter or guide traffic into a safe position.

If the area of diagonal stripes has a solid edge do not enter that area except in an emergency.

The general rule for diagonal white stripes is to ask yourself:
    "Can I avoid driving over that area?"

If the answer is "yes", then do not drive on the stripes.

In some circumstances (parked vehicles/obstructions etc.) you may have to enter the striped area to proceed normally. This would be acceptable. However you **do not** overtake if it would involve driving over an area marked with diagonal stripes or chevrons.

Diagonal white stripes separating streams of traffic:

Used on bends, and at other places of danger, the stripes keep opposing traffic streams apart where they could come into conflict with each other. The striped lines allows a greater

DIAGONAL WHITE STRIPES EXAMPLES OF WHERE THEY ARE USED

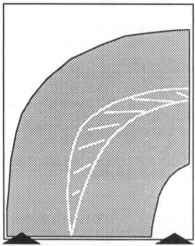

To separate streams of traffic which might endanger each other

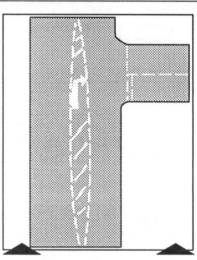

To protect traffic turning right

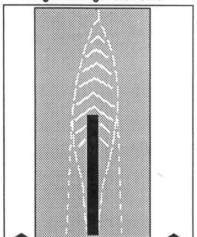

To guide traffic at the end of a dual carriageway

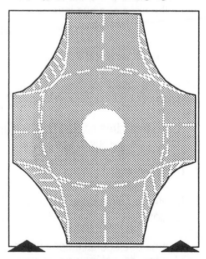

To guide traffic at roundabouts

Diagonal White Stripes Protecting Traffic Turning Right:

Vehicles wishing to turn right are protected by the stripes from possible conflict with vehicles approaching from behind or oncoming overtaking traffic.

There is usually a 'safety-zone' within the striped area and possibly a white painted arrow (pointing right) in the 'safety-zone'; you do not need to position your vehicle exactly on the arrow; it is intended as a guide. In some circumstances you could drive over the striped area to enter the safety zone.

There are some areas of diagonal white stripes that do not have a 'safety-zone' for right-turning traffic. In this circumstance it is acceptable to drive onto the striped area to position your vehicle to turn right. In this situation if you did not move onto the striped area, you would hinder and confuse following traffic.

Diagonal White Stripes Guiding Traffic Into The Safest Position:

When leaving a one-way system (or dual-carriageway) it is necessary for traffic to be guided into one lane. This is so that when the road becomes two-way there is less risk of opposing traffic meeting head on.

As you approach the end of a dual-carriageway the outer lane will be gradually 'shaded' out, using white diagonal stripes.

Diagonal white stripes are also used at roundabouts to guide traffic to a position from where they can take effective observation, or to guide traffic into a single lane or approach where the space around the roundabout might be so restricted as to bring vehicles into conflict.

The above are the main examples of where you will see diagonal white stripes being used.

As a general rule, wherever you see them being used, ask yourself the reason why they are there; it will always be for a good safety related reason.

18.8 Yellow box junctions

These are designed to keep junctions clear and so prevent traffic becoming gridlocked (unable to move in any direction).

The rule for a yellow box junction is:

* You **must not** enter unless your exit is clear.

The only exception to this is if you are turning right and it is only oncoming traffic that is preventing you from turning.

18.9 Other road markings

Words written on the road surface will be self-explanatory:

Slow
Keep clear
Stop
Etc. etc.

Take heed and comply with them at all times.

Cats-eyes: These are rubber studs with two reflective 'eyes', used to mark and separate lanes. Night driving is made easier because the 'cats-eyes' reflect back light from your headlamps, allowing you to see the direction of the road etc.

Dual-carriageway and motorway cats-eyes are coloured.

Red :	Left hand side
Amber :	Right hand side
White :	Separating lanes
Green :	Across acceleration/ deceleration lanes

In fog-prone areas the cats-eyes may be closer together.

18.10 Railway level crossings

Approach a level crossing at a moderate speed and cross it with care. Do not loiter. Never drive "nose to tail" over it. Never drive on to one unless you can see the road is clear on the other side. Never stop on or immediately beyond any level crossing.

Most modern level crossings have steady amber and twin flashing red traffic lights. **Always** obey these traffic lights and stop at the white line if the red lights are flashing. Invariably a train will be coming, and if there are barriers, they will be lowered.

AUTOMATIC HALF-BARRIER LEVEL CROSSINGS

These crossings have automatic barriers across the left hand side of the road. These are operated by the train and lower automatically just before the train reaches the crossing. Amber lights and an audible alarm followed by flashing red "STOP" lights warn you when the barriers are about to come down. Do not move on to the railway once these signals have started - the train cannot stop and will be at the crossing very soon. Wait at the "STOP" line. If you are on foot, wait at the barrier, or the broken white line on the road or footpath. Never zig-zag around the barriers - you could be killed and endanger other lives. If one train has gone by, but the barriers stay down, the red lights continue to flash and the audible alarm changes in tone, you must wait as another train will soon arrive.

If you are already crossing when the amber lights and alarm start, keep going.

If the barriers stay down at any time for more than three minutes without a train arriving, use the telephone at the crossing to ask the signalman's advice.

If your vehicle stalls, or breaks down, or if you have an accident on the crossing:

First : Get everyone out of the vehicle and clear of the crossing; then use the telephone at the crossing immediately to tell the signalman.

Second : If there is time, move the vehicle clear of the crossing. Contact the signalman again to let him know when the crossing is clear. If the alarm sounds, or the amber light shows, get everyone well clear of the crossing.

AUTOMATIC OPEN CROSSINGS

Some level crossings without gates, barriers or attendant have amber lights and an audible alarm followed by flashing red "STOP" lights. When the alarm sounds and the lights show you must stop and wait. Do not cross the railway - a train will reach the crossing shortly. If one train has gone by, but the lights continue to flash, you must wait as another train will soon arrive. The lights will go out when it is safe to cross. At some crossings there is a special sign before the crossing and a special railway telephone at the crossing. At these crossings if you are driving a very large or slow vehicle, or are herding animals, you must first telephone the signalman to make sure it is safe for you to cross. Contact him again to tell him when you are clear of the crossing.

LEVEL CROSSINGS WITH GATES OR FULL BARRIERS

Many level crossings have gates, or barriers with skirts, that are operated either by an attendant or by remote control and go right across the road. Some also have amber lights and an audible alarm followed by flashing red "STOP" lights. Do not pass the lights once they show. If there are no lights at all, stop when the gates begin to close or when the barriers start to descend.

Some level crossings with gates or barriers but no attendant have "STOP" signs and small red and green lights. Do not cross when the red light is showing, as a train is coming. If the green light is showing, open both gates or fully raise both barriers, and check that the green light is still showing before you cross. Close the gates, or lower the barriers when you have crossed. Where there is a special railway telephone at the crossing and you are driving a very large or slow-moving vehicle, or are herding animals, first telephone the signalman to make sure it is safe for you to cross. When you have crossed, telephone the signalman again to let him know you are over.

Some level crossings have gates, but no attendant or red lights. At such crossings, stop, look both ways, listen and make sure there is no train coming. If there is a special railway telephone, first telephone the signalman to make sure it is safe for you to cross. If you have telephoned or not, before crossing with a vehicle or animals, open **both** gates wide and then make a further check that no train is coming. Drive your vehicle or animals clear of the crossing and then close both gates. If you have telephoned the signalman, contact him again when you are clear of the railway.

OPEN LEVEL CROSSINGS

At level crossings with no gates, barriers, attendant or traffic lights, there will be a "Give Way" sign. You must look both ways, listen and make sure there is no train coming before you cross. Always "Give Way" to trains.

18.11 SUMMARY: Traffic signs/ road markings

* Know the different shapes of signs.

* Stop and give way lines.

* Other road markings.

* Cats-eyes.

* Railway Level Crossings.

19

TURNING THE VEHICLE ROUND IN THE ROAD

19.1 Is it a 3-point-turn?

Sometimes, but not always. This manoeuvre is referred to as 'the turn-in-the-road' because it could take more than 3 turns to turn the vehicle round.

The number of turns it takes will depend on the following factors:

* Length of vehicle and turning circle.

* Width of road.

The number of turns will always be an odd number: 3, 5, 7 etc.

On the driving test the examiner will ask you to carry out this manoeuvre by saying to you:

"I'd like you to turn your vehicle round and face the opposite way using your forward and reverse gears. Try not to touch the kerb when you're turning".

If, for example, you were to take the driving test in a larger vehicle (a minibus for example) it might take you 5 turns to turn the vehicle round because of its length and turning circle. This would be acceptable. However, in a smaller (more manoeuvrable) vehicle if you took 5 turns when the manoeuvre could be done in 3, this would be unacceptable because you

obviously had not got sufficient co-ordination of the controls to manoeuvre the vehicle in a confined space.

19.2 Potentially dangerous ...

This manoeuvre is potentially dangerous because you will be crossing 2 lanes of traffic and will not be giving any signals (a signal would be confusing for other road users).

To carry out this manoeuvre safely you need to:

* **Co-ordinate the controls properly**
(Combining the clutch with the gas to drive the vehicle slowly, coupled with rapid steering.)

Note: during this manoeuvre (as with any other in a confined space) the left foot may remain on the clutch throughout to give you the smooth precise control necessary at slow speeds. With your left foot you can control the speed of the car by holding the clutch at the biting point and either 'dipping' (clutch pedal pushed down and held just below the biting point) or raising the clutch a tiny amount-about the thickness of a £1 coin. This is called getting the 'feel' of the clutch and will improve with practice.

THE TURN - IN - THE ROAD

Consider street furniture when carrying out this manoeuvre

Before starting this manoeuvre ask yourself:

- Is it safe ?

- Is it Legal ?

- Is it convenient ?

- Is it within your ability ?

SAFETY FACTORS

- Co-ordinate the controls properly.

- Observation with due regard for all other road users.

- Reasonable accuracy.

Remember also that thin-soled shoes will enable you to get the 'feel' of the clutch better, giving you more precise control of the car. The 'feel' of the clutch will vary from vehicle to vehicle, even on the same model, so do not expect every clutch to feel the same, or 'bite' at the same point.

*   **Observe properly**
    (All round observation)

*   **Be reasonably accurate on positioning**
    (Do not mount kerb, do not drive too far down the road before turning)

19.3 Why? ...

This manoeuvre is designed to demonstrate to the examiner on your driving test that you can manoeuvre your vehicle safely and under control in a confined area with due consideration for all other road users.

Although you may seldom carry out this manoeuvre itself in your driving career it is similar to parking in a car park (multi-storey, supermarket, motorway service area, etc.) so it does, therefore, relate to everyday driving.

You can use the turn-in-the-road as a method of turning your vehicle to go back in the direction you have just come. Say, for example, if you inadvertently drive into a 'no-through-road' or cul-de-sac.

Another method of turning the car round is by reversing into a side road; this will be covered in detail in the next chapter, 20.

19.4 How to ...

Before carrying out this manoeuvre ask yourself:

*   **Is it a safe place?**
    (Not near a junction, bend or anywhere where other road users view of you would be restricted)

*   **Is it convenient?**
    (Not near parked cars or pedestrians [especially children] ... pavements)

*   **Is it legal?**
    (Not in a one-way street, dual carriageway, motorway)

*   **Is it within your ability?**
    (Have you done this manoeuvre on a gradient (up and down) or a narrower road? If, after having stopped, you decide it is not within your ability, use another method of turning your vehicle round (not on your driving test though!)

19.5 Assess the road

Having decided it is safe, convenient, legal and within your ability, you should then look at the road and assess the degree of camber.

The camber of the road is where it slopes down from the crown or middle of the road to the gutters on each side.

The purpose of this camber is to enable water to drain off the road, keeping the surface as clear as possible.

The amount of camber in roads will vary and will need to be assessed when carrying out the turn-in-the-road.

Sometimes this camber can be quite severe or alternatively there may not appear to be any camber at all and the road could be flat and level.

If you have not correctly assessed this slope, you might roll forward (or backward) into, and mount, the kerb which is obviously extremely dangerous to pedestrians but will also damage your tyres.

Even if your tyres just touch the kerb there will be a certain amount of your vehicle overhanging the pavement - again this is dangerous especially if there are children around. Also there may be obstructions (boulders, tree stumps, bollards, etc.) on the pavement or verge, which could damage your vehicle. Where possible, try and stop about 1ft/30cm from the kerb, to avoid the above.

Initially, when practising this manoeuvre it will help you to get a feel for the size of your vehicle, and where the wheels are, if you let your vehicle **gently** touch the kerb when going forward and backwards.

This must be done where there is obviously no danger whatsoever to other road users.

19.6 Method

The sequence for carrying out the turn-in-the-road is as follows:

You may remove the seat belt (because this manoeuvre involves reversing).

1. Select first gear.

2. Observation: interior mirror, door mirror, blind spot, ahead, interior mirror.

3. Release handbrake (assuming start is level; otherwise procedure is for uphill/downhill start).

4. Drive the vehicle forward slowly, steering quickly and fully to the right.

5. Aim at getting your vehicle at a right angle across the road.

6. About 3ft/1m from the kerb clutch down, steer left.

7. About 1ft/30cm from the kerb gently brake to a stop.

8. Apply handbrake.

9. Select reverse gear.

10. Set the gas (more than usual; due to the camber of the road treat this as a hill start).

11. Find the biting point.

12. Observation: look right, left, over your right shoulder and left shoulder.

13. Release the handbrake.

14. Looking over your left shoulder drive the vehicle backwards slowly, steering quickly and fully to the left.

15. As you get over the middle of the road steer to the right and look over your right shoulder. (The back wheel at the right would be the first to touch the kerb.)

16. About 1ft/30cm from the kerb gently brake to a stop.

17. Apply the handbrake.

18. Select first gear.

19. Set the gas (more than usual; due to the camber of the road treat this as a hill start).

20. Find the biting point.

21. Observation: look right, left, then right again.

22. Release the handbrake.

23. If safe drive the vehicle forward slowly, steering to the right, and then steering left to a park position, mirror check, gently brake to a stop.

24. Apply handbrake, select neutral.

25. Replace seat-belt if you have removed it.

Note: As a guideline, try to get full right lock on the steering **before** your car reaches the middle of the road.

The narrower the road, the later you leave it to steer the opposite way.

Remember: speed slow, steering quick.

19.7 Practice makes perfect . . .

Once you have mastered the basic principles of this exercise you should practice it in different types of road:

* Up/downhill gradients.

* Differing cambers.

* Narrower roads.

When practising, consider any residents of the street you are in and limit your practice to 3 on any particular section of road.

Important points to note are:

a) Make sure you check behind over both shoulders **before** the vehicle moves backwards. A common fault is looking forward as the vehicle starts moving; this could be very dangerous - think of children behind the vehicle.

b) **Drive** the vehicle **slowly** but **turn** the **steering** wheel quickly. Only turn the steering wheel when the vehicle is moving. The reason for this is that if the vehicle is stationary and the steering wheel is turned it puts too much strain on the steering linkage and will cause excessive wear and tear, possibly resulting in a dangerous mechanical failure. This applies equally to power steering as well as 'normal' steering.

As a guide, when driving forward you should try and get full right 'lock' (steering wheel turned to the right as far as it will go) by the time the front of the vehicle reaches the middle of the road.

19.8 Other traffic . . .

Although a quiet road will have been chosen for this exercise, there is always the possibility of traffic coming along whilst you are manoeuvring.

You must be prepared to stop and let traffic pass.

If they stop for you make sure it is safe and then continue with the manoeuvre, but do not rush it or you may make mistakes.

It is advisable not to wave traffic past - you could be waving them into danger.

However, if you have vehicles waiting on both sides and one is edging forward impatiently it might be prudent to wave him through and therefore remove the uncertainty.

It should be stressed, however, that you should take all the circumstances into account at the time, and check as clearly as you can in both directions before beckoning to another road user; consider every aspect and weigh up the danger involved. Make sure that your signal (waving or beckoning) is clear and positive.

As in any 'one-off' driving situation, there can be no black or white way of doing things; it all depends on the circumstances at the time. Use your commonsense and make safety your priority.

19.9 SUMMARY:The turn-in-the-road

* Co-ordinate the controls.

* Observation with due regard for all other road users.

* Be reasonably accurate in positioning.

Note: When reverse gear is engaged most vehicles will show one or two white lights to the rear. Do not assume that other road users (especially pedestrians/children) will know this. Think for them and, if necessary (whilst waiting to continue with the manoeuvre), select neutral to switch off the reversing lights and therefore remove any uncertainty other road users may have about your intentions.

The white reversing lights will enable you to see behind when reversing at night. However, unless the road is extremely well lit it would be inadvisable to carry out the turn-in-the-road at night - consider that your vehicle will be broadside on to traffic with no lights immediately visible.

20

REVERSING INTO A LIMITED OPENING TO THE LEFT OR RIGHT

20.1 To the left, or right?

If you take your driving test in a standard car with side windows you will **always** be asked to reverse to the left.

If you were to take the test in a vehicle with limited rearward visibility (i.e. a van, or minibus) you would be asked to reverse to the right. The reason for this is that in a van or minibus your view to the side is severely limited and if you were to reverse to the left you would be unable to judge the point at which you should start turning (the point-of-turn).

However, when reversing to the right you can check your position in relation to the kerb by checking through the side window over your right shoulder.

Although very few people actually take the test in a van or minibus, it is still useful to know how to reverse to the right; you may one day hire a van or minibus and find yourself in a situation where you need to turn the vehicle round.

20.2 Why? ....

This manoeuvre is designed to demonstrate to the examiner your ability to drive in reverse gear, in a straight line, enter a limited opening, straighten the vehicle and continue to drive in reverse gear keeping reasonably close and parallel to the kerb (on the correct side of the road), with due regard to other road users, including pedestrians.

In your driving career, you may seldom find yourself actually carrying out the exercise itself. However, it is very similar to parking in a car park, between cars, so it does relate to everyday driving.

Also it is another method of turning your vehicle round.

20.3 Reversing safely ...

To reverse safely you need to be able to see properly to make sure there are no other road users who will be inconvenienced. You will get a better view behind if you sit a little more sideways in your seat, angled towards the passenger side. You may remove your seat-belt to enable you to do this. If you are unsure about whether there are any obstacles or pedestrians about, ask your passenger to get out and look, or do so yourself (but not on lessons or driving test!) When reversing you must be prepared to

REVERSE INTO A LIMITED OPENING ON THE LEFT

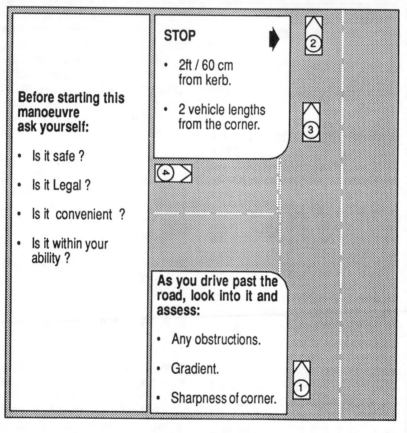

Before starting this manoeuvre ask yourself:

- Is it safe ?

- Is it Legal ?

- Is it convenient ?

- Is it within your ability ?

STOP

- 2ft / 60 cm from kerb.

- 2 vehicle lengths from the corner.

As you drive past the road, look into it and assess:

- Any obstructions.

- Gradient.

- Sharpness of corner.

SAFETY FACTORS

- Co-ordinate the controls properly.

- Observation with due regard for all other road users.

- Reasonable accuracy.

REVERSE INTO A LIMITED OPENING ON THE RIGHT

Before starting this manoeuvre ask yourself:

- Is it safe ?

- Is it Legal ?

- Is it convenient ?

- Is it within your ability ?

As you drive past the road, look into it and assess:

- Any obstructions.

- Gradient.

- Sharpness of corner.

SAFETY FACTORS

- Co-ordinate the controls properly.

- Observation with due regard for all other road users.

- Reasonable accuracy.

stop and give way to all other road users.

To carry out this manoeuvre safely, you will need to:

* **Co-ordinate the controls properly.**

Note: during this manoeuvre (as with any other in a confined space) the left foot may remain on the clutch throughout to give you the smooth precise control necessary at slow speeds. With your left foot you can control the speed of the car by holding the clutch at the biting point and either 'dipping' (clutch pedal pushed down and held just below the biting point) or raising the clutch a tiny amount (about the thickness of a £1 coin). This is called getting the 'feel' of the clutch and will improve with practice. Remember also that thin-soled shoes will enable you to 'feel' the clutch better, giving you more precise control of the car. The 'feel' of the clutch will vary from vehicle to vehicle, even on the same model, so do not expect every clutch to feel the same, or 'bite' at the same point.

* **Observe properly**
  (Before reversing, whilst reversing and forward at point-of-turn.)

* **Be reasonably accurate in positioning**
  (Approx. 2ft/60cm from kerb, parallel to it and on your side of the road.)

20.4 How to . . .

Before carrying out this manoeuvre ask yourself:

* **Is it safe?**
  (Not in busy area, not at crossroads.)

* **Is it convenient?**
  (Consider other road users.)

* **Is it legal?**
  (Not from a side road into a main road - very dangerous.)

* **Is it within your ability?**
  (Have you carried out this manoeuvre up/downhill with different corners - sharp, gradual, etc.?)

20.5 Method (to the left)

On your driving test the examiner will ask you to:

"Pull up on the left before the next road on the left."

The next road is the one he will ask you to reverse into, and he has pulled you up before it so that you can assess it as you drive past it.

The examiner will say to you:

"I'd like you to reverse into the road on the left. Drive past it and stop. Back in and continue to drive in reverse gear for some distance. Keep reasonably close to the kerb."

You should drive on, and as you pass the road into which you are going to reverse, look into it and try and get as much information as possible:

* Any parked vehicle/obstructions?

* Uphill or downhill?

* Sharp or gradual corner?

You should stop (remember the mirror check) about 2 car lengths (8m/24ft) from the corner. Any further is unnecessary and will just make things more difficult for you.

Also, it is illegal to reverse for longer than is necessary.

The distance of 8m/24ft should be sufficient that you can see the apex (tip) of the corner.

You should stop about 2ft/60cm from the kerb: this will lessen any risk of damage to the tyres from any misjudgement with steering, and allow you a margin of error.

The seat-belt may be removed during this manoeuvre, allowing you to turn in your seat to get a better view.

Do not be tempted to remove the head restraints to give a better view. It is up to you to look properly around the head restraint, or any part of the vehicle which obscures your view (a rear spoiler, or passengers, etc.)

If you wear glasses do not be tempted to remove them for this manoeuvre. Sit so that you can look 'squarely' through the rear window. If you are looking at an angle your view could be distorted or obstructed by the frames when not looking through the middle of the lenses.

20.6   Reversing to the left (level road)

Prepare the vehicle: Select reverse gear. No signal necessary - it would only confuse other road users.

Observation: Check forward and behind over both shoulders.

Manoeuvre: Release the handbrake and drive the vehicle slowly backwards, looking over your left shoulder through the centre of the rear window. If you were to watch the kerb through the right-hand side of the rear window   you could find yourself 'drawn' into it. Also you would not get any overall view of the road. By looking through the centre of the rear window you will be able to see any traffic approaching, and be able to stop if necessary.

Glance forward frequently so that you are aware of the traffic situation all around you.

When the back wheels are level with the last straight kerbstone (or the point at which the kerb starts to bend) check forward and over your right shoulder. This observation must be done **before** you start to turn because when you start to turn the front of the car will swing out so you need to check that it will not inconvenience or endanger other road users.

As a guideline, the back wheels are situated directly underneath the top of the rear seat back rest and when that lines up with the last straight kerbstone or point where the kerb starts to bend, that is your 'point-of-turn'.

The amount you steer to the left will depend on how sharp the corner is. Remember that if you need to turn the wheel $1\frac{1}{2}$ turns to the left to get round the corner you will need to turn it $1\frac{1}{2}$ turns to the right to straighten up.

When driving the car backwards keep looking through the centre of the rear window when steering, and steer the way you want the car to go. If you want it to go towards the kerb, steer towards the kerb, and vice versa. When reversing it is the same two wheels that do the steering as when going forwards. However the steering effect is delayed and it will take slightly longer for your steering input to be translated into movement of the car. So you may need to start turning slightly earlier than might seem necessary. By keeping the speed of the car very slow (walking speed) it will give you more time to look and steer, and make adjustments as necessary.

It should be noted that the reverse gear is the lowest gear in any car. This means that it needs the least power to move the car when in that gear. On a level road only very slight pressure on the gas pedal is all that is required, and any slight variation in speed can be obtained by 'dipping' the clutch. This means pushing the clutch pedal down just below the biting point. The effect will be to make the car slow down or, eventually, to roll to a stop. By bringing the clutch back up to the biting point and holding it there, further progress can be made as necessary, when required.

When your vehicle is halfway round the corner, check to the right again.

When you are approximately two-thirds of the way round the corner, start to straighten up and aim to get the back of your car pointing straight down the road. As a guideline, focus about 20m/yds down the road, on a parked vehicle if possible. This will help you to keep the car straight. Do not look at the kerb - you will find yourself 'drawn' into it, and you will be unaware of any approaching traffic.

Drive back for about 4 or 5 car lengths, keeping the car straight and parallel to the kerb. Any minor adjustments to your position should be by slight movements of the steering wheel. Imagine the wheel as a clock face and move it 5 or 10 minutes whichever way you want to go. Any larger movements will cause you to 'weave' as you over-steer one way and then over-correct the other way.

When driving in a straight line make frequent checks forward - two reasons for this:

i) check for other traffic;

ii) check the position of the front of the car in relation to the kerb, to keep the car parallel (both nearside wheels same distance from kerb).

When the examiner wants you to stop driving backwards he will say "Thank you, drive on and at the end of the road turn left/right please."

You should aim to end up with your vehicle 2ft/60cm from the kerb. Gently brake to a stop, apply the handbrake and select neutral. Replace your seatbelt and drive on, obviously carrying out all the necessary checks before moving away.

Do not indicate for your new direction until the car is moving.

When carrying out this manoeuvre, if in misjudgement you find you are driving into the kerb, stop before you actually do, and drive the car forward as necessary to straighten up and move away from the kerb. Then carry on with the reversing manoeuvre. You do not need to ask the examiner, just do it. After all, if you were out driving unaccompanied (Which is what the test is all about) you would have to cope with the situation as best you could. Again commonsense provides the answer - show the examiner you can cope!

However this does not mean that you can spend half of the test shuffling backwards and forwards around a corner until you get it right. That would obviously signify a lack of control.

20.7 Reversing to the left (uphill/downhill)

Uphill: When reversing uphill remember that you will need to use the uphill start technique and will need more gas. Each time you come to a stop, apply the handbrake.

Downhill: When reversing downhill you can control the vehicle with the footbrake, letting the weight of the car, and gravity move the vehicle as necessary. It is important that reverse gear is engaged - the white reversing lights will come on to alert other road users to the fact that you intend to travel backwards; this would not happen if you let the vehicle roll back when in neutral.

With reverse gear selected, hold the clutch right down with your left foot and control the speed of the car with your right foot on the footbrake.

The clutch is held down for as long as the vehicle will travel under its own momentum. If the road levels or goes uphill bring the clutch to the biting point then drive the car backwards. This obviously involves moving your right foot to the gas pedal.

20.8 Practice makes perfect ...

Once you have mastered the basic principles of this exercise you should practice on different corners:

* Level, uphill and downhill.

* Gradual corners.

* Sharp corners.

When practising, consider any residents of the street you are in and limit your practice to 3 on any particular corner.

Important points to note are:

a) Make sure you check behind over both shoulders **before** the vehicle moves backwards. A common fault is looking forward as the vehicle starts moving; this could be very dangerous - think of children behind the vehicle.

b) Keep the speed of the car to a slow walking speed.

c) Look the way the car is going and steer the way you want the car to go.

20.9   Reversing to the right (level road)

You would be asked to reverse to the right if you were to take your driving test in a vehicle with limited rearward visibility. In such a vehicle, this is the safest method of turning the vehicle round.

Even if you do not take your test in a van you may some day hire one and find yourself in a situation where you may need to turn the vehicle round.

On your driving test the examiner will pull you up before the road he wants you to reverse into and will say:

"The next road on the right is the road I'd like you to reverse into. Drive past it and then move over to the right-hand side of the road and stop. Back in and continue to drive in reverse gear for some distance, keep reasonably close to the kerb."

You should drive on, and as you pass the road into which you are going to reverse, look into it and try and get as much information as possible:

* Any parked vehicles/obstructions?

* Uphill or downhill?

* Sharp or gradual corner?

You should stop (remember the mirror check) about 2 car lengths (8m/24ft) from the corner. Any further is unnecessary and will just make things more difficult for you.

Also, it is illegal to reverse for longer than is necessary.

The distance of 8m/24ft should be sufficient that you can see the apex (tip) of the corner.

You should stop about 18"/45cm from the kerb: this will lessen any risk of damage to the tyres from any misjudgement with steering, and allow you a margin of error.

The seat-belt may be removed during this manoeuvre, allowing you to turn in your seat to get a better view.

Do not be tempted to remove the head restraints to give a better view. It is up to you to look properly around the head restraint, or any part of the vehicle which obscures your view (rear spoiler, passengers, etc.)

First you must assess the start; level, uphill or downhill? Each of these will be explained.

20.10 Reversing to the right (level road)

Prepare the vehicle: Select reverse gear. No signal necessary - it would only confuse other road users.

Observation: Check forward and behind over both shoulders.

Manoeuvre: Release the handbrake and drive the vehicle slowly backwards, looking over your left shoulder through the centre of the rear window. By looking through the centre of the rear window you will be able to see any traffic approaching, and be able to stop if necessary.

If in a van make fullest use of the door mirrors, and physical checks over your right shoulder.

Glance forward frequently so that you are aware of the traffic situation all around you.

When the back wheels are level with the last straight kerbstone (or the point at which the kerb starts to bend) check forward and over your right and left shoulder. This observation must be done **before** you start to turn because when you start to turn the front of the car will swing out so you need to check that it will not inconvenience or endanger other road users.

As a guideline, the back wheels are situated directly underneath the top of the rear seat back rest and when that lines up with the last straight kerbstone or point where the kerb starts to bend, that is your 'point-of-turn'.

The amount you steer to the right will depend on how sharp the corner is. Remember that if you need to turn the wheel $1\frac{1}{2}$ turns to the right to get round the corner you will need to turn it $1\frac{1}{2}$ turns to the left to straighten up. When driving the car backwards keep looking through the centre of the rear window when steering, and steer the way you want the car to go. If you want it to go towards the kerb, steer towards the kerb, and vice versa. When reversing it is the same two wheels that do the steering as when going forwards. However the steering effect is delayed and it will take slightly longer for your steering input to be translated into movement of the car. So you may need to start turning slightly earlier than might seem necessary. By keeping the speed of the car very slow (walking speed) it will give you more time to look and steer, and make adjustments as necessary.

It should be noted that the reverse gear is the lowest gear in any car. This means that it needs the least power to move the car when in that gear. On a level road only very slight pressure on the gas pedal is all that is required, and any slight variation in speed can be obtained by 'dipping' the clutch. This means pushing the clutch pedal down just below the biting point. The effect will be to make the car slow down or, eventually, to roll to a stop. By bringing the clutch back up to the biting point and holding it there, further progress can be made as necessary, when required.

When your vehicle is halfway round the corner, check all around again.

When you are approximately two-thirds of the way round the corner, start to straighten up and aim to get the back of your car pointing straight down the road. As a guideline, focus about 20m/yds down the road, on a parked vehicle if possible. This will help you to keep the car straight. Do not look at the kerb - you will find yourself 'drawn' into it, and you will be unaware of any approaching traffic.

Drive back for about 5 or 6 car lengths, looking over your left shoulder but with glances forward and to the right, keeping the car straight and parallel to the kerb. Any minor adjustments to your position should be by slight movements of the steering wheel. Imagine the wheel as a clock face and move it 5 or 10 minutes whichever way you want to go. Any larger movements will cause you to 'weave' as you over-steer one way and then over-correct the other way.

When driving back in a straight line make frequent checks forward - two reasons for this:

i) check for other traffic;

ii) check the position of the front of the car in relation to the kerb, to keep the car parallel (both offside wheels same distance from kerb).

When the examiner wants you to stop driving backwards he will say "Thank you, drive on and at the end of the road turn left/right please."

You should aim to end up with your vehicle 12"/30cm from the kerb. Gently brake to a stop, apply the handbrake.

Replace your seat-belt and drive on, returning to the correct (left-hand) side of the road. Obviously carry out all the necessary checks before moving away.
Do not indicate for your new direction until the car is moving.

When carrying out this manoeuvre, if in misjudgement you find you are driving into the kerb, stop before you actually do, and drive the car forward as necessary to straighten up and move away from the kerb. Then carry on with the reversing manoeuvre. You do not need to ask the examiner, just do it. After all, if you were out driving unaccompanied (which is what the test is all about) you would have to cope with the situation as best you could. Again commonsense provides the answer - show the examiner you can cope!

However this does not mean that you can spend half of the test shuffling backwards and forwards around a corner until you get it right. That would obviously signify a lack of control.

20.11 Reversing to the right (uphill/downhill)

Uphill: When reversing uphill remember that you will need to use the uphill start technique and will need more gas. Each time you come to a stop, apply the handbrake.

Downhill: When reversing downhill you can control the vehicle with the footbrake, letting the weight of the car, and gravity move the vehicle as necessary. It is important that reverse gear is engaged - the white reversing lights will come on to alert other road users to the fact that you intend to travel backwards; this would not happen if you let the vehicle roll back when in neutral.

With reverse gear selected, hold the clutch right down with your left foot and control the speed of the car with your right foot on the footbrake.

The clutch is held down for as long as the vehicle will travel under its own momentum. If the road levels or goes uphill bring the clutch to the biting point then drive the car backwards. This obviously involves moving your right foot to the gas pedal.

20.12 Practice makes perfect ...

Once you have mastered the basic principles of this exercise you should practise on different corners.

* Level, uphill and downhill.

* Gradual corners.

* Sharp corners.

When practising, consider any residents of the street you are in and limit your practice to 3 on any particular corner.

Important points to note are:

a) Make sure you check over both shoulders **before** the vehicle moves backward; A common fault is looking forwards as the vehicle starts moving backward; this could be very dangerous - think of children behind the vehicle.

b) Keep the speed of the car to a slow walking speed.

c) Look the way the car is going and steer the way you want the car to go.

20.13 Other traffic

Whilst reversing you must be prepared to stop and give way to all other road users including pedestrians. Remember to give way to pedestrians who are already in the road when you turn a corner; this applies when travelling backwards as well as forwards.

If traffic approaches when you are reversing around the corner you must stop and wait. If necessary, drive forward to a position where you will not get in the way. Use commonsense and take proper observation before moving forward or continuing the reverse manoeuvre.

Remember, when reversing, it is you who is doing the extraordinary thing and you must not endanger or inconvenience any other road user.

Never reverse for longer than is necessary; it is illegal.

20.14 Summary: reversing into a limited opening to the left or right

* Co-ordinate the controls.

* Observation with due regard for all other road users.

* Be reasonably accurate in positioning.

Note: When reverse gear is engaged most vehicles will show one or two white lights to the rear. Do not assume that other road users (especially pedestrians/children) will know this.

Think for them and, if necessary (whilst waiting to continue with the manoeuvre), select neutral to switch off the reversing lights and therefore remove any uncertainty other road users may have about your intentions.

The white reversing lights will enable you to see behind when reversing at night. If your vehicle is not fitted with reversing lights you could illuminate the road / garage / driveway immediately behind by switching on your rear fog lights, brake lights or even indicator. However take particular care not to mislead other road users.

21

21.1 Definition

Parking is generally when you leave your vehicle unattended.

You will generally park:

* Off-street
  (In your drive/garage, car park: multi-storey, pay/display, other.)

* On-street
  (By the kerb/at meters/ . . .

Before you park, consider the following factors:

* Is it safe?

* Is it convenient?

* Is it legal?

21. 2 Off-street parking (driveway/garage)

When parking in a driveway it is generally safer and more convenient to reverse into it.

This applies especially if you live on a busy road; it is much easier to manoeuvre forward to join the traffic flow. Your visibility will be much better as well.

When reversing into a driveway or garage, follow the sequence as described in chapter 20. Remember the following:

Control the vehicle **slowly.** This, together with precise **steering** will enable you to be reasonably accurate whilst maintaining **proper observation** with due regard to other road users.

Bear in mind though, that, unlike reversing around a corner, if you were to hit something it will not be a kerb that you hit but a gate post or wall or a garage wall (or even another car).

So you will see how important it is to control your vehicle slowly.

Do not become complacent if this is a manoeuvre you perform every day, say when going to and returning from work.

There have been cases where parents have driven over their own children in their own driveway. So each time **before** reversing make sure you check properly behind the car. If necessary get out and look.

Incidentally, when parking in driveways or garages ensure that you leave sufficient space for you to open your door to get out.

Before entering the driveway or garage it is advisable for passengers to leave the car; this will save them from perhaps having to squeeze out, and will also enable you to have an unobstructed view - remember that passengers can cause blind spots which you cannot see through.

When in a garage do not leave the engine running for longer than is necessary - there will be a build-up of fumes from the exhaust. These fumes are noxious and inhalation of them should be avoided where there is insufficient ventilation.

When moving away from your own driveway make sure you check your blind spot(s). Again, do not become complacent just because you drive off every day and there is nothing there. Always check, and if your vehicle is exposed on the other side, check over your left shoulder as well.

When parking in your driveway or garage always 'park pretty'. This means parking with your wheels straight and the steering wheel straight. The reasons for this are:

* Parking with your front wheels sticking out can endanger or inconvenience other people.

* If the wheels were not straight, and you inadvertently start the car in gear, it could jump forwards (or backwards) into a wall.

Even when parked in your own driveway or garage lock all the doors, boot, etc., and if you have an alarm, set it. Do not assume your car is safe just because it is on your property. Lock it or lose it.

Discourage young children from running out to greet someone returning or visiting. If you have them, keep gates closed to prevent young children running onto the road.

21. 3 Parking behind a single parked vehicle

You may be asked to demonstrate this manoeuvre on your driving test. Please note that it will always be behind a single parked vehicle - never between two parked vehicles.

The examiner will say to you: "Would you pull up on the left well before you get to the next stationary vehicle please.

This is the reverse parking exercise. Will you drive forward and stop alongside the vehicle ahead. Try to keep the two bonnets level and parallel.

Then reverse in and park reasonably close to, and parallel with, the kerb. Try to complete the exercise within about two car lengths from that vehicle.
Start when you're ready please."

After carrying out your observations, you should drive on and checking the mirrors, pull up alongside the stationary vehicle and about 3ft/1m from it.
Remember to use the P.O. M. routine, so:

Prepare the car; select reverse gear:

Observation: Check forward and behind over both shoulders. If clear...

Manoeuvre: Looking over your left shoulder (through the middle of the back window), drive the car backwards slowly using clutch control.

When the back of your vehicle is level with the stationary vehicle (this is the point-of-turn) so observation must be carried out:

Check forward and over your right shoulder (Remember that the front of the car will swing out) and also check into the space behind the stationary car.

As you drive *slowly* backwards, steer to the left approximately 1 turn of the steering wheel, (practice and experience will guide you); it is important to note that by driving slowly you will give yourself time to look and steer, making corrections as necessary.

When your passenger door mirror (or windscreen pillar) is level with the corner of the stationary car, steer approximately 1 turn to the right; frequent glances around will enable you to assess the traffic situation.

Then, as the front left corner of your vehicle passes the corner of the stationary vehicle, steer to the right to bring the front of your car in towards the kerb. As you get closer to the kerb steer slightly left.

Finally, shunt the car forwards and backwards so that you are 'parked pretty', with nearside wheels close to and parallel with the kerb. Don't park too close to the stationary vehicle - leave sufficient room, ie: you can see the wheels and some of the road

Having achieved competence in this exercise, you can then go on to practice parking between two vehicles.

21. 4 Parking in between two vehicles (at the kerbside) - level road

This is also called parallel (to the kerb) parking using reverse gear.

Before carrying out this manoeuvre ask yourself:

* Is it safe?
* Is it convenient?
* Is it legal?
* Is it within your ability?

Look for a gap that is $1\frac{1}{2}$ - 2 times the length of your vehicle. If the gap is larger than 2 car lengths you could drive in frontwards, thereby causing less of an obstruction or hazard to passing traffic. However, when manoeuvring in smaller gaps (2 car lengths or less) it is easier to reverse in.

This is because:

* The back wheels do not steer and you can therefore position the 'non-steering' end in a small gap and then pull the front (steering end) into the gap.

* Reverse gear is the lowest gear and enables the car to be manoeuvred more smoothly and precisely in confined areas.

REVERSE PARKING

Initially, practice parking behind a single parked vehicle. When you are competent at this, practice parking between two parked vehicles on the left, and on the right (in a one-way street)

Checking mirrors, stop alongside (allowing a gap of 3ft/1m), and parallel to, the stationary vehicle. Try to get the two bonnets level (be prepared to adjust the position of your car to take into account varying vehicle size, and road width etc).

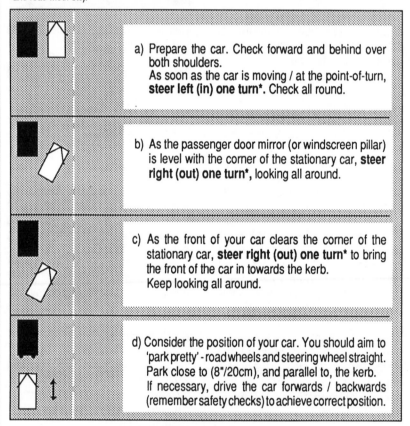

a) Prepare the car. Check forward and behind over both shoulders.
As soon as the car is moving / at the point-of-turn, **steer left (in) one turn***. Check all round.

b) As the passenger door mirror (or windscreen pillar) is level with the corner of the stationary car, **steer right (out) one turn*,** looking all around.

c) As the front of your car clears the corner of the stationary car, **steer right (out) one turn*** to bring the front of the car in towards the kerb.
Keep looking all around.

d) Consider the position of your car. You should aim to 'park pretty' - road wheels and steering wheel straight. Park close to (8"/20cm), and parallel to, the kerb. If necessary, drive the car forwards / backwards (remember safety checks) to achieve correct position.

SAFETY FACTORS
- Co-ordinate controls properly.
- Observation with due regard for all other road users.
- Reasonable accuracy.

*NOTE: Use as a guideline only; if you drive the car slowly (walking pace) this will give you time to look and make any steering corrections that may be necessary.

146

Drive past the gap and stop alongside the vehicle behind which you are going to park. Keep about 1m/3ft from it and parallel to it, with bonnets level if possible.

Observation: Check forward and behind over both shoulders and in your mirrors.

Manoeuvre: Looking over your left shoulder (through the middle of the back window), drive the car backwards slowly.

When the back of your vehicle is level with the vehicle you have stopped alongside, check forward and over your right shoulder (remember that the front of the car will swing out).

Looking through the middle of the back window, drive the car very slowly steering to the left to manoeuvre the back of your vehicle into the gap. Aim your rear nearside wheel at a point on the exposed kerb, midway between the two vehicles.

Frequent glances forward will enable you to assess the traffic situation ahead of you.

As the front of your vehicle passes the end of the vehicle you have stopped alongside your nearside (passenger) back wheel should be approximately 2ft/60cm from the kerb. Start steering to the right. As you do this check that the nearside (passenger) front corner of your vehicle is adequately clearing the other vehicle. As you clear this vehicle steer to the right to swing the front of the car in towards the kerb.

As you get closer to the kerb steer slightly left.

From the driving seat, check your distance from the kerb and the two vehicles and adjust your vehicle's position by driving forwards and backwards as necessary. Ideally you should park 6" - 8" (15 - 20cm) from the kerb and be centrally positioned between the two vehicles. Do not scuff (rub or scrape) your tyres against the kerb; this can damage or weaken the tyre wall, with possibly dangerous consequences later on: blow out, puncture, etc.

In some residential areas, parking is permitted on the kerb, or pavement. This is done in order that the (usually) narrow roads do not become blocked with parked vehicles. An additional hazard in this case is that you will have to drive your car up onto the kerb - you will need to use more gas to do this (the amount will depend on the size of the kerb). Be careful to immediately relax the pressure on the gas pedal when your wheel has mounted the kerb.

Where parking on the kerb is allowed, it will be indicated by signs on lamp posts or poles. On adjacent roads where there is no kerb parking, the sign will have a red bar through it.

When carrying out this manoeuvre you may remove your seat belt.

If you are carrying out this manoeuvre in a street with shop windows, you can use the reflection to aid your parking. However, do not forget to check all around as well.

21.5 Parking in between two vehicles (at the kerbside) - uphill or downhill

Where possible, avoid parking on a hill. It is more difficult and you need more room.

If it is unavoidable, remember that when reversing uphill you will need to use the uphill start technique, and every time you stop you will need to apply the handbrake.

Reversing downhill into a parking space would require the use of downhill start technique.

Engage reverse gear (to illuminate your reversing lights and let other road users know of your intentions) and with the clutch pushed fully down, and held down, use your right foot on the footbrake to control the speed of the car.

21.6 Practice makes perfect . . .

When parking, remember that you will become more proficient with practice, so do not feel discouraged if at first you do not succeed!

It can be impractical to practice parking in between parked vehicles because:

* You will be causing an obstruction.

* You may not find a suitable gap.

* It might annoy residents.

However, you can practice parking in the following way:

* Practice parking behind a single car; pull alongside a single parked vehicle and reverse park parallel to the kerb within a distance of $1\frac{1}{2}$ to 2 car lengths. Your instructor will be able to accurately judge the distance.

By practising this you will gain confidence and be able to become more accurate in positioning your vehicle.

Having achieved a certain competence parking behind a single vehicle, you can then go on to practice parking between two parked vehicles.

However, consider that some vehicle owners may not feel too pleased at having their vehicles used for practising on, so use your discretion and do not practice continually between the same two cars!

21. 7 Off-street parking (car parks)

When you enter a multi-storey, underground or indoor car park, switch on your dim-dip lights (or side lights) so that your vehicle can be seen.

Be aware that people will be walking to and from cars, possibly wheeling shopping trolleys and will be more intent on going home (or controlling a wayward trolley) then on looking out for cars!

Unless you find a space at the end of a row of parked cars, you will have to park in a gap between two other cars.

It is generally better to reverse into such a gap, making it easier for you to drive out.

When parking ensure that you allow sufficient clearance between your car and the cars on either side. Remember that you and your passengers will need to open doors and so will the drivers and passengers of adjacent cars.

If you are driving a two-door car you should allow greater clearance on each side. This is because on two-door cars the doors are longer and you will need to open them wider to get out of the car.

When parking in a parking bay remember to 'park pretty' and square the car up, with the front wheels straight, and steering wheel correctly aligned.

Car parks have different lay-outs and methods of paying:

* Pay on entry.
  (Make sure you have a selection of coins in the car.)

* Pay and display.
  (Pay at machine and display ticket in car.)

* Pay before exit.
  (Keep your ticket when leaving the car and pay on foot at machine to obtain exit ticket. Place ticket in machine at exit to raise barrier.)

* Pay on exit.
  (Put money in machine at exit to raise barrier/pay attendant in kiosk.)

On entry to a car park read all the notices and obey them, taking particular note of payment instructions, after all you do not want to arrive at the exit barrier and find that you have no change! The drivers of the cars behind you would not be amused! Also be aware that some car parks close at certain times.

When parking in large multi-storey car parks (and airport car parks) make sure you make a note of the exact location of your car (floor number and position), otherwise you could spend a great deal of time wandering between floors, 'convinced' that you were parked in a certain spot!

Having parked, remember to switch off your lights, and lock all doors and boot. Any valuables in the car should be hidden from view or locked in the boot. If you have a car alarm fitted, activate it.

21.8 SUMMARY: parking safely, allowing adequate clearance

To carry out this manoeuvre safely, you should:

* Co-ordinate the controls of the vehicle properly.

* Observe with due regard for all other road users. **especially pedestrians.**

Park squarely, think of other drivers/ pedestrians.

* In car parks, note any restrictions.

* Always lock your car and use the alarm, if fitted.

22

DRIVING IN ADVERSE WEATHER CONDITIONS / NIGHT DRIVING

22. 1 What are adverse weather conditions?

Any one or combination of the following could be classified as adverse weather:

* Rain (standing water)/wet roads (spray)/floods

* Snow/ice/black ice

* Fog

* Frost

* Hail

* Low winter sunshine

* Cross winds

The worse the conditions the slower your speed, in any conditions that reduce visibility keep all windows clean and clear. Drivers who wear glass/contact lenses should make sure that they are also clean.

22. 2 Driving in rain . . .

When driving in rain take the following precautions:

* Use wipers to keep screen clear (and rear screen).

* Slow down

* Keep a greater distance between yourself and any vehicle you are following (remember on a wet road your stopping distance is doubled).

* Use dipped headlights if visibility is reduced (make sure other road users can see you).

In rain your view from inside your vehicle will be reduced due to rain on the windows and exterior mirrors. Obviously it will help if all windows and mirrors are kept clean and clear inside and out.
The inside of your windscreen and other windows may mist up. Use the ventilation system to clear the windows. Opening the side windows a tiny amount (10cm/$^1/_2$inch) will ensure that air is circulated throughout the car, helping to reduce misting.
A thorough knowledge of your vehicle's heating/ventilation/air conditioning/climate control will enable you to get the best out of it. Study your vehicles's handbook to learn how to operate it.

Make sure you wipers are in good condition - do they clear the screen effectively or do they leave areas uncleared?
Consider changing the wiper blades. Your windscreen washer reservoir

should be topped up as necessary; adding a cleaning agent will help to remove flies and other stubborn marks.

Remember that when it is raining pedestrians can dash across roads, more interested in keeping dry than road safety! People with umbrellas may not look properly (if at all) when crossing the road. Anticipate this and if necessary use a horn signal to alert them to your presence.

22.3 Surface water . . .

Be especially careful when rain has dampened a road after a long dry spell - it can make the road extremely slippery due to rubber, dust and oil deposits combining with water.

Be aware that water can collect at the side of the road and form pools of standing water.

Driving into these pools may wrench the front wheels out of line and cause the driver to lose control.
Take particular care at night, when the difference between a wet road surface and flood water is difficult to detect. Water will also collect in dips in the road (under a bridge for example) and in low lying areas.

Avoid driving through pools of water - there may be obstacles (bricks, broken bottles) or even pot-holes, which you cannot see.
Drive around the affected area (with due consideration to all other road users), but if this is not possible drive through the shallowest part. Consider

pedestrians and do not inconvenience them by driving through puddles close to them.

If the road is completely flooded stop and assess the situation.
Consider the clearance that your vehicle's engine will have (especially electrical components).

Having decided to drive through, you should:

* Select first gear and . . .

* Set the gas, have the engine running fast and keep it like that. (By doing this, water will be prevented from entering the exhaust pipe).

* Drive forward slowly through the water, maintaining a slow steady speed. This will be achieved by 'slipping' the clutch (keeping just at or below the biting point, to keep the speed very slow).
If you go too fast you will cause a bow wave which could flood the engine and cause you to stop.

* Once you have driven through the flood, dry your brakes by driving slowly with your **left** foot pressing lightly on the brake pedal until the grip increases. Do this again after a short time to ensure the brakes are fully effective.

Fords . . .

A ford is where a stream passes over a road. The depth can vary considerably - look for a depth gauge at the side. Consider that there may be boulders/rocks, etc., under the surface. Drive through as for floods. Having driven through, dry your brakes.

22. 4 Surface water (aquaplaning)

What is aquaplaning?

Aquaplaning literally means 'riding on water' and happens when the wheels lose contact with a wet road surface at speeds of approximately 50 m.p.h. or more.

The tread pattern on tyres must disperse a certain amount of water if contact between the tyre and road surface is to be maintained. If the amount of surface water is excessive or the speed of vehicle is excessive, or your tyres are worn, then the tyres cannot disperse the required amount of water and will ride on top of the water: aquaplaning. This is extremely dangerous as you will have no steering control and braking will make the situation worse. If your vehicle is front wheel drive you will not be able to accelerate.

If you suspect your vehicle is aquaplaning, or is about to, you should ease off the gas to slow the vehicle down. **Do not brake.**

Control will only be restored when your tyres have regained contact with the road surface. (When aquaplaning your steering will suddenly feel very light.)

Aquaplaning can occur:

* In heavy rain, where there is a film of water over the road.

* Speeds of 50 m.p.h. or more.

* On a badly drained or smooth road.

* If tyres are worn.

Remember: you have no control over the road surface, but you can control your speed - slow down in the wet.

22. 5 Surface water (spray)

In rain, or on a wet road surface spray will be thrown up by other vehicles, reducing your vision, so keep your distance in order that you can see beyond the vehicle.
The larger the vehicle, and the more wheels it has, the greater the amount of spray it will throw up. This will also increase with speed.
On motorways anticipate this hazard from large vehicles and adjust your wiper speed (double if possible) to cope with the expected spray from these larger vehicles as you pass them or they pass you.

22. 6 Snow

When driving in falling snow or on fallen snow you must:

* Slow down.

* Increase the gap between yourself and the vehicle in front.

* Use wipers/demisters as necessary.

* Use dipped headlights.

Be aware that snow may pack around wheel arches, affecting steering and brakes. Keep all lights clear. Stop and clean them and the windscreen as necessary.

Use the accelerator and brake gently and smoothly. Plan well ahead to avoid harsh braking. Do not brake on corners or bends. Snow can obscure road marking and road signs so take particular care at junctions.

In continued snowy conditions keep sacking in the car to provide grip if you get stuck. A shovel could come in handy as well.

22. 7   Ice / black Ice

On icy road surfaces allow up to ten times the stopping distance.

Use all controls very delicately and smoothly. Avoid harsh steering, braking or acceleration.

Do not brake on corners or bends. Use the gears as an aid to braking - select lower gears earlier than you would normally.

Black Ice

Black ice is caused by rain freezing on the road as it falls. The road may look wet but can be sheet ice. If your speed is excessive on black ice the steering will feel light and the back end of the car may start to drift. **Do not brake:** ease off the gas to slow the vehicle down.

Note: When driving on ice, tyres will make virtually no noise, so in circumstances when ice may occur, switch off other sources of noise - radio, tape player, etc., open your windows a small amount to enable you to detect changes in road surface noise. If the road you are travelling on appears wet, it may turn to ice and the road noise from the tyres will decrease becoming almost noiseless; drive with the utmost caution - slow down well in advance of any hazard, using deceleration (foot easing off gas), selecting lower gear earlier, and very gentle braking as necessary.

22. 8   Fog

When it becomes foggy or you run into fog, you should:

* Slow down.

* Increase the gap.

* Use wiper/demisters/heated front screen if fitted.

* Use dipped headlights/front fog lights.

* Use rear fog lights if visibility is reduced to less than 100m.

* Do not hang on to the tail lights of the vehicle in front.

* Take particular care when driving in fog at night.

* Watch your speed - you could be going faster than you think.

Fog can vary in thickness and can be very patchy - you can be driving in sunshine one minute and then in a patch of thick fog the next.

Be alert to the conditions and plan ahead. When emerging from a clear patch or when the fog has cleared, do not forget to switch off your lights, especially rear fog lights. Fog can be disorientating, do not stare fixedly ahead - blinking will stop you doing this.

At junctions in fog open your windows and listen for other traffic. When waiting keep your foot on the brake pedal to put your brake lights on. This will give extra warning to following traffic.

Right turns in fog are extremely dangerous and should be avoided if at all possible

Before starting a journey in fog ask yourself "Is it necessary?". If it is, allow extra time.

Note: Fog can make well-known surroundings seem strange and unfamiliar - objects will appear to 'loom' out of the fog, and then disappear quickly. This effect can be disconcerting if you have not experienced it before.

Fog will also deaden sound making everything seem very quiet.

When driving at night in fog it is inadvisable to use 'full beam' headlights as the light will reflect back from the fog, with no increase in vision. Use dipped headlights and front fog lights if fitted.

22. 9 Frost

If your vehicle is parked outside during the winter months it could be covered in frost in the mornings. Before driving away ensure that you clear all windows **properly.** Be prepared to stop, if necessary, to clear the windows again. Make sure you have a de-icer spray, and a scraper.

It is not sufficient to scrape a small patch to look through - this is extremely dangerous, Be careful of other drivers who may be driving like this! Assume that they cannot see you and keep your distance!

Although frost on the road can quickly disperse with morning sunshine, be aware that shaded areas can remain frosty for much longer periods, possibly all day.

On a bright frosty morning, just because you are warm inside your car, do not get lulled into a false sense of security. The roads could still be frosty and slippery. Other road users (pedestrians, cyclists and motorcyclists) will be affected by the cold weather, so make allowances for them and give them extra clearance.

22. 10 Hail (pellets of frozen rain)

Hail storms occur when there is a sudden drop of temperature and falling rain turns to hailstones, which can vary in size from peppercorn to golf ball! Hail storms are usually short but severe and in the space of a few minutes can cause absolute chaos.

The sudden drop of temperature will cause the windows to mist up, so make the fullest use of demisters and heated rear screen .

Hailstones falling onto the car sound very loud indeed.
This noise can be disorientating and, if you have not experienced it before, can be frightening.
Visibility will also be severely reduced.

When encountering a hail storm you should:

* Slow down
  (If visibility is very severely restricted stop in a **safe** place to let it pass - it will not usually last long.)

* Use dipped headlights and rear fog lights.

* Use wipers (front and back), demisters and heated rear window/ front screen, and open side windows slightly.

Within the space of a few minutes the road surface can become carpeted with hailstones which makes it extremely slippery.

Hail storms are infrequent but happen very suddenly and usually without warning - do not panic, keep calm and follow the advice above.

22.11 Low winter sunshine

To minimise the dangers from this, make sure all windows are clean and clear, **inside** as well as out.
Keep a clean, unscratched pair of sun glasses in the car, readily to hand.

Make use of the sun visors - anticipate the sun when changing direction or coming over the brow of hill.
By anticipating this hazard and having your sun visor in place, you will avoid fumbling with one hand off the wheel when you turn into the sun.

If you cannot see, slow down and keep your speed down until you can.

If low winter sunshine is directly behind you, it can dazzle in your interior rear view mirror. If this happens 'dip' your mirror to reduce the dazzle. If your mirror does not have a 'dip' facility, move your head slightly to avoid being dazzled.
Because of this dazzle, vehicles approaching from behind may be 'lost' in the sun. Take particular care therefore when changing lanes/ overtaking when such conditions prevail.
Having clean windows (**especially the insides of the windows**) will prove beneficial by allowing you maximum vision, and reducing glare.
Be aware that sunshine reflecting off a wet road surface will cause glare and can also cause road-markings (white lines) to be temporarily obliterated.

22.12 Strong winds

Especially noticeable on exposed rural roads and motorways/dual carriageways, strong winds can rock the car from side to side making it difficult to keep on a steady straight course.

Keep a firm grip on the steering wheel - slow down as necessary. You will have to correct the steering constantly to counteract the effect of strong winds.

Strong winds affect other road users:

* Cyclists/motorcyclists will wobble or swerve or may be blown off course; so allow them plenty of room.

* Pedestrians may have trouble maintaining their balance and may be walking with their heads down and may not see road traffic. Again, allow them extra clearance and consider that they could dash into the road,

Note: In windy conditions be very careful when opening car doors, either getting in or out. A strong gust of wind could snatch open the door, flinging it wide open. This would obviously cause extreme danger to passing vehicles, especially cyclists and motorcyclists. In these conditions use two hands to open, keep hold of, and steady the door.

Remember that large vehicles (especially high sided) will be affected more than cars, so give them a wide berth and allow them plenty of room. Caravans (being lighter) will also be affected and can even be blown over.

Strong winds can seriously reduce your speed (to the extent that you might think there is something wrong with your car) and affect handling - steering will seem heavier. Fuel consumption will increase because of the extra power needed to maintain headway.

Be aware that in tree-lined roads, branches may be blown into the road. Other debris such as dustbins, dustbin lids, boxes, etc., etc., may end up in the road.

When parking outside, always park so the front of the car is not facing directly into a strong wind - it could affect starting and, if raining, it would blow the rain onto the engine and/or electrical components, making starting even more difficult.

22.13 Stubble burning

Stubble burning usually occurs in August/September when farmers burn the stubble left in their fields following harvesting.

If the field happens to be next to a major road or motorway, the resulting thick black smoke can be as dangerous as fog; it can drift over a road causing visibility to be severely reduced.

Quite often stubble burning will happen on bright warm, sunny days. Because of this such a hazard is usually quite unexpected and many drivers are unprepared, resulting in confusion and panic braking with possible disastrous consequences.

From 1992 there will be a ban on stubble burning. This is because the resulting smoke can cause accidents, and is a severe nuisance to anybody in the vicinity.

If your route takes you through farmland where stubble burning could occur, take the following actions if you encounter thick black smoke across the carriageway:

* Slow down

* Use dipped headlights and **rear** fog lights.

* Keep windows closed when driving through (smoke inside the car would affect your eyes and lungs).

Note: In hot summer weather there may be fires on the embankments of motorways, etc., causing black smoke. Follow the advice above.

22. 14 Night driving

Switch on your headlamps when visibility is reduced. Switch on earlier if you have a dark coloured vehicle. Make sure your headlamps are correctly adjusted and will not dazzle other road users.

Keep your lights clean at all times. Accumulated dirt on your headlamps seriously reduces their effectiveness to the point where you might think they are not working at all!

Most filling stations have a bucket and sponge so when you stop for petrol use the opportunity to clean your lights. Obviously this is more important in rain, fog, snow, muddy conditions, etc. Also, make sure all windows and windscreens are kept clean and clear - especially the inside of the windows (a film can build up,

reducing your vision).

Do not use tinted glasses when driving at night as these can reduce the contrast between light and dark making obstructions less visible. Allow time for your eyes to adjust to the dark especially if you are coming from a brightly lit area; for example, from home or the office. Remember that your eyesight will deteriorate with age and it will take longer for your eyes to adjust from light to dark and vice versa. This will also apply if your eyesight is already defective in any way (i.e. if you wear glasses or contact lenses).

At night, never drive so fast that you cannot stop within the range of your own lights. When following other traffic use dipped headlights and make sure that you are far enough back so that your dipped beams fall clear of the vehicle (this is so that you do not dazzle the driver).

Only use full beam headlamps where they would not dazzle other road users (this includes cyclists/motorcyclist and pedestrians).
On unlit country roads the lights of other vehicles will warn you of their approach - make sure you dip your lights in good time. Dip earlier going round a left-hand bend, because your headlamp beams will sweep across the eyes of anyone coming towards you.

When driving at night it is more difficult to judge speed and distance because you have less information to enable you to work out a vehicle's approaching speed or size. Also at night be aware that cyclists and motorcyclists will be even more difficult to see.

It is more tiring driving at night because you need to concentrate harder. Because of this, on long journeys you may need to take more frequent breaks.

When stopping at night (for example to let passengers in or out) switch off your dipped beam headlights. The reason for this is that the fixed glare of **stationary** headlamps can be very dazzling. When stopped use your dim/dip lights or side lights. However when moving off do not forget to switch your dipped beams back on.

When parking and leaving your vehicle at night ensure that it is legally parked.
Consider residents and do not slam doors, rev your engine or do anything else which would cause a nuisance.

NOTE: At night orange street lights can cause white lines and road markings to become almost invisible, especially if the road surface is wet, so under these circumstances take particular care.

22. 15 SUMMARY: adverse weather conditions

* Slow down!
  (Consider increased stopping distances, etc.)

* Make sure you can see properly.
  (Keep all windows clean and clear.)

* Be aware of changes in the weather and plan your drive accordingly.
  (i.e. fog into sunshine.)

The worse the conditions, the slower your speed.

REMEMBER - YOU CANNOT CHANGE THE CONDITIONS BUT YOU CAN CHANGE YOUR SPEED.

23

SKIDS
(HOW TO AVOID THEM)

A skid is when the tyres lose contact with the road surface and the vehicle either swings out or slides along the road.

23. 1 How are skids caused?

By the driver.

Cars do not skid by themselves. The driver makes a car skid.

Any driver who says: "It wasn't my fault, the car skidded on the icy road", is really saying that he did not adjust his driving to suit the conditions.

Remember: Weather and road conditions cannot be changed. Your driving can.

23. 2 When will skids happen?

The risk of skidding increases when the grip between the tyres and the road surface is lessened.

The conditions affecting this grip are:

* Wet road surfaces.

* Ice/snow.

* Frost (in shaded areas).

* Loose gravel.

* Wet leaves.

* Mud.

* Oil (possibly from spillage).

In any of the above conditions if a car is driven at a steady speed there will be no skid.
However, when a driver changes his speed or direction the risk of skidding increases:

* Slowing down or speeding up.

* Turning corners or bends.

* Travelling uphill or downhill.

Obviously, in normal driving you will be doing any or all of the above to suit speed limits, road and traffic conditions,

The car will skid when the driver is asking more from the car in terms of braking/acceleration and/or steering than is possible with the amount of grip that the tyres have on the road at the time.

If you think that the road surface is slippery, keep your speed down. Use deceleration (ease off gas) and very gentle braking. Select lower gears earlier than you would normally.

159

The most effective way of controlling skids is to drive in such a way that you will avoid them.

Maintaining your car in good condition will also reduce risks.

* Make sure brakes stop evenly, without pulling to one side.

* Make sure that the accelerator pedal linkage operates smoothly and easily. If it is stiff or jerky it could cause wheel spin.

* Make sure tyres have good tread depth.

Note: The legal requirement regarding tread depths is as follows:

* Tyres must have at least 1mm of tread across 3/4 of the width, and around the complete circumference.

* Tyres must also have a visible tread pattern on the remaining $\frac{1}{4}$ of the tyre.

* Bald or worn patches will render a tyre illegal.

23.3 Correcting skids

If you brake very hard and lock the wheels (wheels stop turning) you will skid in a straight line or veer to one side or the other.

Obviously this would be extremely dangerous on a bend - instead of travelling around the bend you would either plough into a hedge or wall, or into the path of oncoming traffic.

Remember that with the wheels locked you will have no control over the steering of the car and therefore the direction.
To enable you to steer around an object or person you must release the footbrake (when the wheels have locked) so that the tyres can grip the road.
The footbrake should be used with a firm 'pumping' action to bring the car to a stop.
This 'pumping' action is necessary on roads where grip is reduced. As soon as the wheels lock, you have little or no control over the car.

The brakes are at their most effective just before they lock. By releasing the pressure on the footbrake at this point you will avoid locking the brakes. Then re-apply the pressure, releasing and re-applying as necessary to stop the vehicle. Also, by 'pumping' the brakes the weight of the vehicle will be thrown forward, onto the front wheels, also helping to brake.

In vehicles fitted with A.B.S. (anti-lock braking systems) the task of applying and releasing is done electronically many hundreds of times per second, to enable you to concentrate on control of the car and steer out of danger.

If the back of the car skids out - swings either to the left or right - you should steer into the skid to try and straighten up the car (bringing the front and back wheels into line). Easing off on the gas will help as well.

Try not to overcorrect a skid, as this can then lead to another skid in the opposite direction.

23.4 SUMMARY: skids, how to avoid them

*   Be alert to the road and weather conditions.
    (You cannot change these, but you can change your driving).

*   Whatever the type of skid ease off gas/brake to regain steering control.

*   Steer into a skid to straighten the car.

24

ACCIDENTS: HOW TO AVOID GOING HOME IN A BLACK BIN-BAG

24. 1 Why a black bin-bag?

If you are involved in a road traffic accident and end up scattered all over the road your remains will be gathered in a black bin-bag to be take to the morgue,

Not a very pleasant thought, is it?

Nor is the fact that 5,000 people are killed on the roads each year, every year.

5,000 killed per year, every year.

417 per month, every month.

14 per day, every day.

i every 2 hours.

There are also 64,000 serious injuries (those requiring hospital detainment). Road accidents are a national tragedy and a **preventable** tragedy.

24. 2 National tragedy

Most people will remember the following national tragedies:

ZEEBRUGGE
March 1987   188 dead

CLAPHAM
December 1988   36 dead
HILLSBOROUGH
April 1989   95 dead
MARCHIONESS
August 1989   51 dead

However, the total number of people killed in the above tragedies is **less** than the number of people killed **each month** on the roads.

We all express shock at tragedies such as the above because of the large numbers killed at the same time. However, it is just as much a tragedy even though, because road accidents are spread out throughout the UK, with usually not more than 1 or 2 deaths occurring at the same time, the impact is lessened. It is usually only with a 'sensational' motorway accident that the press report it. By recognising how and when accidents happen you can reduce the risk of being involved in an accident.

24. 3 How are accidents caused?

Human error.

The driver.

You.

The driver is the cause of 95% of all accidents. The remaining 5% is made up with mechanical failure and environmental failure.

Statistics are gathered for any accident involving personal injury occurring on the public highway (including footways) in which a road vehicle is involved and which becomes known to the police within 30 days of its occurrence. The vehicle need not be moving and it need not be in collision with anything.

Because of all the information gathered it is possible to see patterns emerging; where and when accidents happen and which road users are most at risk.

24. 4 Who is involved in accidents?

The most recent accident figures available (1990) show that there were:

* 340,100 injury accidents (932 per day).

* 5,104 fatalities.

* 60,435 serious injuries.

Road Users	Numbers Killed	Most at risk
Pedestrians	1,636	Under 15 $\frac{1}{2}$ over 60 yrs
Pedal cyclists	238	Age 10 - 14
Motorcyclists	650	Age 17 - 24
Car users	2,349	Age 18 - 24
Goods vehicle users	191	(males 60% more at risk)
Others	18	Age 18 - 24
Total	5,082	

Road users most at risk on road (in order) based on fatalities per 100 million kilometres.

* Motorcyclists.
* Pedestrians - (21% of all casualties occur in London.)
* Pedal cyclists.
* Car users.

Note: All of the above figures relate to 'injury' accidents. Damage only accidents are not recorded but obviously there are very many of them.

Source:
Road accidents GB 1990, HMSO.

24. 5   Where do accidents happen?

Accidents can, literally, happen anywhere. However, most fatal accidents occur:

* In built-up areas (30 mph limit)
  (More pedestrians / cyclists / motorcyclists, greater density of traffic.)

* On major single carriageway roads where national speed limit applies (60 mph).
  (Traffic travelling at higher speeds - any accident is therefore more severe.)

Most accidents happen:

* Turning right or waiting to turn right.
  (Twice as many accidents happen leaving a main road, as entering a main road.)

* Going ahead on a bend.

* Waiting to go ahead but held up.

* Overtaking a moving or stationary vehicle.

It will be seen from this that junctions present the biggest hazard to road users. This is because road users join, meet and cross, causing possible conflict.

24. 6   When do accidents happen?

The winter months, October, November, December, have the highest accident rate.

Fridays are the worst days for accidents, with an increase in accidents per day starting from Sunday.

The reason that Thursdays, Fridays and Saturdays produce higher accident figures is that there is more activity - people going shopping, going out for the evening, etc.

A factor which particularly affects male drivers is that young drivers are more likely to have an accident in the evening. Accident rates peak between 10 p.m. and midnight for male drivers aged 17 to 20. However, this peak disappears entirely after the age of 28.

24. 7   Under the influence . . .

About 30% of all people killed in road accidents had alcohol levels above the legal limit for driving.

The legal limit is:

   35 micrograms of alcohol per 100 millilitres of breath.
   80 milligrams of alcohol per 100 millilitres of blood.
107 milligrams of alcohol per 100 millilitres of urine.

Alcohol affects different people in different ways, but the one consistent factor is that it will affect your driving in the following ways:

* Takes you longer to react.

* Reduces your co-ordination.

164

* You are less able to judge speed and distance and assess risk.

* You will feel overconfident and able to deal with anything. This will make you a danger to yourself and all other road users.

Driving above the legal limit means losing your licence for a long period and can mean a heavy fine or imprisonment. Also, when your ban has ended you will find it extremely difficult to get insurance cover and the premium could be anything up to ten times the amount you would pay had you not got a Drink Driving conviction.

Do not be tempted to 'just have one drink'.

If you are driving, the only safe course is not to drink alcohol at all. Do not ever feel pressured into drinking alcohol - it is quite acceptable to consume non-alcoholic drinks.

If you are going out with a group of friends, take it in turns to be the driver and stay dry.
Alternatively arrange to get a taxi home. Do not ever get into a car with a driver who has been drinking - do not risk your life through someone else's selfishness.

Be aware that at pub closing times there may be drivers (and pedestrians) on the roads who are 'over the limit'. Look out for clues which will indicate this and keep well clear.

Drinking and driving is selfish - it can ruin lives. If you want to drink, don't drive. Do not put yourself in any situation where that is compromised. Plan ahead and make arrangements for taxis, lifts with 'dry' drivers, etc.

On Friday and Saturday nights between 10 p.m. and 4 a.m. two-thirds (66%) of drivers and riders killed had alcohol levels above the legal limit.

More than one thousand people are killed each year as a result of drinking and driving - that is the equivalent of 3 jumbo-jets full of people . . .

Young and inexperienced drivers or those who drink infrequently will be seriously impaired well below the legal limit.

Note: Alcohol takes a variable amount of time to be eliminated from the body; factors affecting this are:

* Amount of alcohol drunk.

* Type of alcohol (beer, spirits, etc.)

* Whether anything was eaten.

* Build of a person.

In reality this can mean that after a heavy drinking session the previous evening, a person could still be over the limit when he goes to work at 7 a.m. the next morning.

BOTTLE-TO-THROTTLE

How long before driving?

Airline crews have an 8 hour 'bottle-to-throttle' deadline. This means that they drink no alcohol for a minimum of at least 8 hours before flying (for safety reasons).

Use this 'bottle-to-throttle' time as a realistic guideline when you have been drinking and intend to drive the following day,

24. 8 Drugs

Never drive if you are under the influence of drugs or medicines. They can make you feel drowsy and seriously affect your driving ability.

If you are taking prescribed medicines ask your doctor if it is safe for you to drive. Do not under-estimate the effect of drugs or medicine on your driving.

24. 9 Illness/tiredness

Both of these can increase the risk of accidents. If you have 'flu or even a heavy cold, your senses will be affected (vision, hearing, etc.) and your reactions will be slower. If you feel unwell, do not drive.

Tiredness can also slow down your reactions and lessen your concentration: you will be sluggish in your movements and less aware of what is going on around you.
If you are on a long journey and feel tired, stop and have a coffee, or walk around the car, or even have a short sleep. If you feel tired, do not just press on regardless. You could fall asleep whilst driving and not wake up . . .

24. 10 What is the possibility that you will be involved in an accident?

During a standard driving career (age 17 to 70) the probability is that 47% of male drivers and 29% of female drivers will be involved in car accidents.

Of those who are, 28% of males and 16% of females will be involved in at least two accidents.

Ask around your family and friends. It is very likely that some or all of them will at some time have been involved in an accident. Ask them what was the cause, and the effect . . .

24. 11 The consequence of accidents

The most disastrous ultimate consequence of an accident is death, either yours or another road user. Serious injuries could cause you to take time off from work, with subsequent serious financial loss.

Less seriously, your car may be damaged. This will involve you in getting quotes to get it repaired and then time off the road while it is repaired.

This all causes inconvenience and costs you money (hire cars/transport costs). Your insurance premium could increase and if you were found to have committed an offence you could acquire penalty points on your driving licence which again could increase your insurance premium.

It will therefore be seen that an accident can cause death or injury with the obvious consequences to the family involved, and also severe financial hardship.

The cost to rate-payers/poll tax payers of road accidents is £5 **billion** per year. The cost of a fatality is calculated at £$\frac{1}{2}$ million.

If you consider that 95% of accidents could be prevented, this would result in a saving of a vast sum of money which could be put to more constructive use - more money for education/health service?

Ultimately road accidents cost you money. Increased insurance costs mean higher transport costs - most consumer goods are delivered by road. These increased costs are passed on to the consumer - you.

The cost of the emergency services, police/ambulance/fire brigade and hospital treatment is funded by the rates or poll tax. Obviously the cost to the emergency services of accidents is reflected in the rates/poll tax. Again the person who pays is you.

24. 12 Why do accidents happen?

A major factor in road accidents is the attitude of the driver and the behaviour of the driver.

You may have noticed how other drivers have an attitude of:

* "I've got a bigger faster car, so get out of my way."

* "I'm late for an appointment, so get out of my way."

* "I want to get home, move out of the way."

* "You're holding me up, get out of the way."

* "I'm on the main road, I've got right of way. Move!"

* "I've been driving for 25 years, so I know all about driving."

* "I assumed that because the lights were on green, it would be clear."

These are just a few examples of attitude which can lead to accidents. You can probably think of many more.

Why are these attitudes dangerous?

Being selfish is not a good thing in itself but a selfish driver is positively dangerous, because other people are affected. An angry driver is a dangerous driver - even a momentary loss of temper can have disastrous and far-reaching effects.
If someone 'cuts you up', do not retaliate by trying to do the same to

them. This would be a very negative attitude. Be positive and consider how you could have avoided the situation - perhaps by better observation or awareness.

When driving:

* Do not become impatient with other road users.

* Do not become irritated or angry if another driver 'carves' you up.

* Do not allow outside worries - work/school/home, etc., to distract your concentration.

* Keep in-car distraction to a minimum - loud music can lessen your concentration and block out sound from other road users. Be ready to drop out of any in-car conversation in order to concentrate.

* Use and develop all your senses:

Sight: Be aware of what is happening all around you, not just to the front. Develop your peripheral vision (to the sides, on the fringes of your vision) so that you are aware of other road users pulling alongside of you.

Hearing: At junctions or anywhere your vision is restricted, use your hearing to alert you to the approach of other road users. Especially important in fog.
Listen out for any 'unorthodox' noises from your car and consider their meaning.

Perception: Assessing and recognition of hazards.

Look for clues that will alert you to possible dangers - children playing on the footpath, people getting off a bus, etc. etc.

Be aware of the manoeuvres that put you most at risk (see 24.5) and be aware of the most vulnerable road users (see 24.3).

Note: It should also be noted that you must keep your eyes on the road at all times. It is very obvious but it is not generally realised how much ground a vehicle will cover in a second:

At	In one second you will travel
30 mph	45ft/15m.
40 mph	60ft/20m.
50 mph	75ft/25m.
60 mph	90ft/30m.
70 mph	105ft/35m.
80 mph	120ft/40m.
90 mph	135ft/45m.
100 mph	150ft/50m.

As a reference point, it would take you at least 1 or 2 seconds to look at your radio/tape player, or to turn to a passenger or pick something up from the floor, and you can see from the table above just how far you would travel in that time.
Also remember that your eyes will have to re-focus from far to near and vice versa. The older you are and the weaker your eyes, the longer this will take.

Although you may drive with care, consideration and courtesy, there is always 'the other guy'.

A good driver will allow for others' mistakes, and will plan ahead with regard for what others may do and any difficulties they may encounter.

Do not accept signals given by other road users at face value. Look for clues that will confirm an action he is indicating for.

For example, a vehicle indicating right. Is he in the correct position to turn right, is there a turning on the right? etc. etc. What if he cannot complete the turn? etc. etc.

Always consider:

* What you can see.

* What you cannot see.

* What you might reasonably expect to happen.

An example is a ball bouncing out from behind a parked vehicle into the road.

You can see the ball.

What you cannot see is the children, hidden by the vehicle.

You might reasonably expect that the child(ren) will run out into the road.

Having considered the possibility of this you would then slow down and take the necessary action.

Remember that you could be involved in an accident which is no fault of your own. Even though any damage may be covered by insurance, it is very likely that you will be caused inconvenience and possible hardship.

Avoid putting yourself in any situation where your safety is compromised in any way.

However if you are involved in an accident, or are first on the scene of an accident, you should:

1. Warn other traffic by whatever methods are available to you:
   Red warning triangle.
   Hazard warning lights.
   Get someone to warn approaching traffic.

2. Arrange for emergency services (send a bystander) - be as precise as possible with regard to casualties, number of vehicles involved, and location (remember that time could be crucial).

3. Unless casualties may be at further risk of injury, do not move them.

4. Get any uninjured people out of the vehicle and to a safe place.

5. Wait at the scene until the emergency services arrive. Be prepared to give your details to police/fire/ambulance, etc. on request.

6. When practical, note down details: date, time, conditions, other vehicles, etc. If you have a camera handy, photograph the scene from various angles. Remember that your memory will become less distinct as time passes.

If you or your vehicle were involved, do not admit liability or say anything which could be interpreted as that,

such as "I'm sorry". This could invalidate your insurance claim, leaving you personally liable.

Obviously, in any accident involving personal injury, casualties must be looked after as much as possible until professional help arrives.
Get into the habit of carrying a first aid kit in the car. Consider learning first aid from :
St John Ambulance Brigade,
Red Cross,
St Andrews Ambulance Association.

24. 13 First aid at the scene of an accident

If breathing has stopped:

Mouth-to-mouth resuscitation. Remove any obvious obstructions in the mouth. Keep the head tilted backwards as far as possible - breathing may begin and the colour may improve. If not, pinch the casualty's nostrils together and blow into the mouth until the chest rises; withdraw, then repeat regularly once every four seconds until the casualty can breathe unaided.

If unconscious and breathing:

Movement may further damage an injured back, so only move if in danger. If breathing becomes difficult or stops, treat as in foregoing paragraph.

If bleeding is present:

Apply firm hand pressure over the wound, preferably using some clean material without pressing on any foreign body in the wound. Secure a pad with a bandage or length of cloth. Raise limb to lessen the bleeding provided it is not broken.

Reassurance:

The casualty may be shocked, but prompt treatment will minimise this; reassure him confidently; avoid unnecessary movement; keep him comfortable and prevent him getting cold; ensure he is not left alone.

Give the casualty NOTHING to drink.

24. 14 SUMMARY: accidents

* Be aware of why accidents happen.

* Consider vulnerable road users.

* Reduce distractions, outside worries, etc.

* Keep your temper!

* Drive within your limitations and the limitations of the vehicle and the road.

* Change your driving to suit changing conditions.

* Do not ever drink and drive.

* Do not drive if you are unwell or tired.

Note: By the year 1999 the Department of Transport would hope that the accident figures will have been reduced by 30%. The Department can help to improve road safety by improving junctions, installing lights, or roundabouts, etc. However much the Department of Transport do though, it is still up to road users to develop and maintain the correct attitude and be able to recognise and deal with risk situations.

25
GOING SOLO
(AFTER YOUR TEST . . .)

25. 1 " . . . You've passed!"

Well, after all the effort you (and your instructor) have put in, at last you pass your test!

Now what!

Firstly you will need to send off for your full licence. Do this as soon as possible.

You will need to send off:

* Completed licence application form (D1).

* Your provisional licence.

* Your pass certificate (D10).

You do not need to send any money if you are exchanging a provisional licence with pass certificate for a full licence. All necessary details (where to send, etc.) are on the licence application form.
Under normal circumstances you should get your full licence within 3 weeks.

You can drive in the period between sending off for your licence and receiving it.

It is advisable, however, to photocopy both your provisional driving licence and pass certificate before sending them off.

Please note that you will not be able to accompany learner drivers until you have held a full British driving licence for three years and must be at least 21 years of age.

These conditions allow newly qualified drivers to gain experience before accompanying learner drivers.

Your full British licence will be valid until your 70th birthday. Six weeks before your 70th birthday you will be sent a form inviting you to renew your licence. Assuming that you can still satisfy the requirements (health/ eyesight, etc.) you will be sent another licence valid for a further 3 years; after which you will need to re-apply every 3 years.

If at any time during your driving career your health or eyesight deteriorates or you become disabled, consult your doctor or optician as to whether you should continue driving. It is the responsibility of the driver to inform DVLC of any changes.
Remember that it is an offence to drive with uncorrected defective eyesight, or under certain medical conditions.
It should be noted that you must be 18 to drive abroad (see driving abroad).

Hire car companies will not usually hire vehicles to drivers under 21 (age limit may be higher), or to drivers who have held a full licence for less than 1 year. However, if a driver can arrange his own insurance cover they may consider it.

25. 2 Driving on your own . . .

The first time you go out driving on your own, choose a quiet time during daylight hours.

You may feel very conscious of the fact that you have just passed your test, and may feel that everybody is watching you and somehow knows that you have just passed! Do not worry, all new drivers feel like that, just relax and drive the way you have been taught, and before too long you will be enjoying your new-found independence!

Follow a route that you know well (perhaps a route you followed when learning)and keep within an area that you know.

The most obvious difference will be that you will have to decide for yourself which way to go, and also make all decisions yourself with no one to tell you if it's right or wrong.

Initially keep your solo drives to 20 minutes to $\frac{1}{2}$ hour, to build up your confidence when driving alone.

If you will be driving to work, have practice runs outside of rush-hour times, so that you can get used to any particular hazards or road layouts.

Make sure you are familiar with the car you will be driving and know where all the controls are.

The first time you drive to work, allow yourself more time and plan in advance where you are going to park (will you need any particular coins, permit, etc.)

25. 3 Longer journeys . . .

Before going on a longer journey consider the route you will be taking. Plan your route using an up-to-date (check publication date on title page) road atlas and write down the route so that you or a passenger can refer to it on the journey (at a suitable opportunity). Calculate how long it will take you and then allow an extra * 15% for stoppages, hold-ups, etc. When driving long distances do not drive for longer than 2 hours without a break (fatigue can be gradual, so even if you do not feel tired, stop anyway).
Fatigue can kill, so keep the car well ventilated and stop and rest or have a walk/coffee break. Because of the extra concentration required at night, you will tire sooner so take this into account when planning a journey.

Journey times will vary enormously due to various factors:

* Time of day.
  (Rush hour, school times, etc.)

* Weather conditions.
  (Allow extra time for delays.)

* Roadworks/hold-ups, etc. (Check with motoring organisations about your route.)

Consider whether you will need to refuel and, if so, where will you do it. Motorway service stations can be far apart (especially on the M25) so plan ahead.

Note: If you are a female travelling alone on a longer journey, let family/friends know of your departure and arrival time and probable route and on arrival phone to say that you have arrived safely. If you are delayed for any length of time, phone to say so.

25. 4 At the filling station . . .

Make sure you study your vehicle's handbook before visiting a filling station.

You will need to know:

* What type of fuel?
  (Petrol/unleaded petrol/diesel.)

* Which side is the filler cap?
  (Generally diver's side, but check.)

* Does the filler cap need a key, or is it unlocked or released from inside the car?

* How much fuel does the vehicle hold? (Gallons and/or litres.)

When you drive into a filling station, keep your speed down, think of pedestrians.

If possible, pull up with the pump on the side where your filler cap is. However, if this is not possible due to other vehicles, pull up at the nearest available pump which dispenses the fuel you require; most fuel pumps will reach to the other side of your car. If the pump you are at dispenses different types of fuel, check that you press the button for the correct type. Do not overfill as the fuel can overflow and splash your clothes or shoes.

When you have filled up, replace and lock (if applicable) your filler cap, note the amount to pay and pump number and go to the shop or kiosk to pay.

Do not leave your keys in the car or the car unlocked whilst you pay. Before driving away from a filling station, check over **both** shoulders; remember there could be vehicles moving from both sides, and pedestrian movement all around.

Also at the filling station you could:

* Check/refill your windscreen washer reservoir.
  (Most filling stations have a water tap and watering can.)

* Clean your windscreen.
  (Most filling stations have a bucket/sponge.)

* Check your tyre pressures.
  (Look in your handbook for the correct pressures.)

Note: When checking tyre pressures try and do so at the same filling station each time. This is because different air lines can give slightly different readings, so always try and use one particular air line.

Some air lines are free, but some will require a token or coin.

25. 5 At the car wash . . .

Before using an automatic car wash make sure that your vehicle is suitable. At the entrance to a car wash there will be a notice informing drivers of any particular restrictions on using it. Having decided that your vehicle is suitable, go to the shop/kiosk and buy a token for the car wash.

When leaving your vehicle to buy the token, do not leave it with the keys inside, or unlocked. Lock it, even if you leave it for only a few minutes. It only takes a few minute for someone to steal your car or valuables from it.

Before going through the car wash retract the radio aerial, remove the car phone aerial (if fitted) and close the sunroof and all windows.

After emerging from the car wash, check your door mirrors and adjust as necessary - the car wash rollers

may have knocked them out of alignment.

25. 6 Driving abroad

If you are thinking of driving abroad in Europe the minimum age is 18.

When driving abroad it is advisable to get a 'green card' from your insurance company.

Note: Although green it is more likely to be paper than 'card'.

A 'green card' is an extension of your insurance policy to give you the same cover when driving abroad that you have in the UK.

Although not compulsory it is strongly recommended because if you do not have this 'extension', your insurance cover will be limited to the legal minimum of whichever country you happen to be in.

Allow at least 14 days for the issue of a 'green card'. The cost is variable depending on age, type of cover, vehicle, etc. etc.

Be aware that some countries will require you to have an international driving licence. These are issued by the AA/RAC.

Plan any journey well in advance and consult the AA/RAC as to regulations concerning the country or countries that you are planning to visit.

Headlights will need to be adjusted and spare parts organised/insurance cover arranged. Again the AA/RAC will advise on this.

25. 7 "Phone me in the car" . . .

Car phones are becoming more and more commonplace and although they are very useful for business people 'on the road' it must be remembered that safety comes before a call.

If you are driving you must not use a hand-held telephone handset whilst your vehicle is moving. This is because to do so you would have to take one hand off the steering wheel, seriously reducing control.

However, most car phones have a 'hands-free' facility which allows you to speak into a fixed microphone (usually on the windscreen pillar, or sun visor) whilst 'on the move', keeping both hands on the wheel.

If you are using this facility though, do not get so involved in a conversation that your attention is distracted from the road.
If conditions demand your full attention, do not answer the car phone. Most car phones can be programmed to divert to another phone number after so many rings. If fitted, use this facility to divert a call to an answerphone, where any message can be retrieved at a more suitable time.

If you stop to answer a car phone, make sure that you stop somewhere where it is safe, convenient and legal.

Always make sure you know how to operate any equipment fitted in the car, i.e. phone, radio/tape players, etc., **before** driving. Study any relevant literature and practise using the phone, radio/tape player, etc., whilst the car is stationary; when moving, any distraction to your driving must be kept to a minimum.

25. 8 Freedom!!

When you pass your test you will be driving to work, to visit friends, to go shopping, to go to the coast, etc. etc.

Once you pass your test the emphasis on driving will change.

All the time you have been learning to drive the only reason for you being in the car was to concentrate fully on driving the car.

Having passed your test, driving becomes secondary to whatever purpose you are using the car for: going to work, going to a business meeting, etc., and so becomes a means to an end.

Although driving may assume this secondary purpose, do not forget that safety must be your first concern whenever you are driving; your safety and that of all other road users.

Driving can be very enjoyable and there are many ways that an interest in motoring can be furthered and developed.

Many motor racing circuits run courses for saloon sports/racing cars, enabling you to experience speed in a safe controlled environment.
Some circuits also have skid-pans or skid control cars.
There are several schools in the UK that offer 'rally' driving courses which offer authentic rally driving conditions with experienced instructors.

Some Police driving schools run 'better driving courses' which are open to the public. After some theoretical classroom lectures, you are given the opportunity to be driven by a Police instructor. The standard of driving demonstrated is of an exceptionally high standard and will show to you just how smoothly and safely a vehicle can be driven, even at higher speeds; also a running commentary will be given, noting all hazards and stating what action will be taken.

If you ever get the chance to be driven by an expert in any driving field, take it. The experience will make you realise just how far skilful driving can be taken, and give you a target to aim for.

25.9 Carrying passengers. . .

Passengers in the car will affect the handling due to the extra weight. This will be noticeable when braking (it will take longer) and turning (the car will 'roll' more). Also, consider that passengers can obscure your view and could distract you. You **must not** carry passengers in such numbers or in such a manner as is likely to cause danger.

25.10 Carrying loads . . .

Always make sure that any loads carried are properly secured so that neither danger nor nuisance is caused by its falling or by being blown off, or shifting.

25. 11 SUMMARY: after your test

* Initially, keep to roads you know.

* Drive at quieter times to get used to driving unaccompanied.

* Get to know your car thoroughly.

* Plan longer journeys.

* Familiarise yourself with filling station procedure.

* Car phones - safety comes before a call.

* Although driving may become a means to an end make sure safety is you first concern.

* Passengers - do not overload the car.

26
DUAL CARRIAGEWAY AND MOTORWAY DRIVING

26. 1 Definitions

Dual carriageway - a road with a central reservation or division and two or more lanes in each direction.

The national speed limit on dual carriageways is 70 m.p.h., unless signposted lower.

26. 2 Driving on a dual carriageway

There are no restrictions as to which type of traffic may use a dual carriageway.

However, be aware that some dual carriageways can become motorways, which do have restrictions - no 'L' drivers for example. So, be aware of this and keep an eye out for signs to direct you so that you do not join the motorway.

Dual carriageways provide a means of fast travel which is relatively safer - the central reservation means that you will not encounter traffic from the opposite direction.

However, dual carriageways do have junctions, roundabouts, traffic lights, zebra and pelican crossings and even, when traversing rural areas, may have light controlled cattle crossings!

Because the traffic will be moving much more quickly than in built-up areas it would be inadvisable to practise on dual carriageways until your instructor felt that you were competent to do so.

Remember that, although the speed limit may be 70 m.p.h., a lot of drivers disregard this and may be travelling at speeds up to 120 m.p.h.! This means they are covering 180ft/50m per second; also, as a new driver you may find it more difficult to judge higher speeds which means a dangerous situation can develop much more quickly.

26. 3 Which lane?

There is no 'fast lane', 'slow lane' or 'cruising lane' .

When driving:

Keep to the left, position your vehicle centrally in the lane.
If traffic in the inside lane is moving more slowly you may use the middle lane (of a 3 lane dual carriageway) but move back to the inside lane when possible.

Do not drive in the middle lane when you could be driving in the left-hand lane.

The right-hand lane of a dual carriageway is for overtaking only - move back to the middle and the inside lane as soon as you can, but without cutting in.

The following vehicles are not allowed to use the right-hand lane of a carriageway with 3 or more lanes (unless due to exceptional circumstances):

* Goods vehicles over 7.5 tonnes.

* Any vehicles drawing a trailer.

* Buses longer than 12m/40ft.

When turning right from a dual carriageway use the mirror/signal/ manoeuvre routine and making sure that you signal in good time (remember the higher speeds of following traffic) and position yourself to the right in good time.
If necessary, stop in the gap in the central reservation (making sure that you are clear of both carriageways). Obey any road markings in the gap - the general rule is to keep to the left in the gap.

If you cross or turn right into a dual carriageway treat each half as a separate road.
If there is insufficient space in the central gap for the length of your vehicle, wait in the side road until you can cross the dual carriageway in one movement.

26. 4 Traffic joining

When you are travelling on a dual carriageway and you can see a vehicle waiting to join the dual carriageway from a junction on the left, it is helpful to move over to the right-hand lane to allow the other driver to join without unnecessary delay. Only do this though if you can safely move over to the right.

When coming off a dual carriageway remember to adjust your speed.
After travelling at higher speed it can feel as though you are going very slowly when reducing to 30 or 40 m.p.h.

Check your speedometer to make sure you are not exceeding the speed limit.

At the end of the dual carriageway you will see signs warning that two-way traffic is straight ahead.

26. 5 Motorways

Definition: A motorway is a dual carriageway with certain restrictions:

* No pedal cycles.

* No 'L' drivers (except H.G.V.)

* No pedestrians.

* No motorcycles under 50 c.c.'s.

* No animals.

* No agricultural vehicles.

* No invalid carriages under 5 cwt. unladen.

Motorways are safer because the traffic is all moving in the same direction and there are:

* No ordinary junctions.

* No traffic lights.

* No roundabouts.

* No sharp bends.

26. 6 Motorway restrictions

There are certain things you must not do on a motorway:

* Do not exceed the speed limit.

* Do not reverse.

* Do not stop on the carriageway.

* Do not stop on the hard shoulder (except in an emergency).

* Do not stop on, or cross, the central reservation.

* Do not walk on the carriageway.

* Do not make a U-turn.

26. 7 Is your vehicle up to it?

Before using a motorway make sure that your vehicle is capable of travelling at sustained higher speeds. Consult your handbook and check that your tyre pressures are correctly set for high speed travel and/or loads (if carried).

Check fuel (if you run out on the motorway and have to call a garage out it is very expensive) and make sure you have sufficient for your journey.

Consistently higher speeds will wear the engine and other parts. Constant vibration can literally shake loose nuts, bolts, connections, etc. etc., - all the more reason to keep your vehicle in good mechanical order. A break down on the motorway can be very dangerous, expensive and inconvenient and should be avoided at all costs.

26. 8 Facts about motorways

"M-way Horror Fireball Inferno"

Despite headlines like the above, motorways are the safest roads in Britain.
However, when accidents do occur they tend to involve more vehicles and are therefore more 'sensational', which attracts press attention.

The first stretch of motorway was built in 1958 when there were no speed limits! And very little traffic.
At that time there were only 8 million vehicles on the roads, as compared to 23 million today. This figure is growing by an average of 5% so by the year 2000 there will be 29 million vehicles on the road.

Motorways currently account for 1% of the total road miles in the UK., yet they carry 15% of all the traffic!

Over the 10 years 1990 - 1999 the Department of Transport aim to implement a motorway building/widening scheme costing £12 billion. There will be 230 miles of new motorway built and 500 miles of existing motorway will be widened to cope with larger volumes of traffic.

The busiest motorway is the M1 and on certain sections of that the traffic volume is frequently as high as 150,000 vehicles per day, far in excess of the expected volume of traffic.

26. 9 Joining a motorway ...

Generally you will join a motorway from a slip road. The final 300m/yds or so of this slip road is called the acceleration lane.

The purpose of the acceleration lane is so that you can build up your speed to match that of the traffic on the motorway.

Also, from the acceleration lane, you will be able to see traffic on the motorway and judge when to join. Use the mirror/signal/manoeuvre routine. If there is no suitable gap in the traffic, wait in the acceleration lane.
Do not drive along the hard shoulder or push your way into the traffic stream.

26. 10 Driving on the motorway

When driving on a motorway, keep to the left.

When you first join the motorway stay in the left-hand lane until you have acclimatized yourself to travelling at speed, getting the 'feel' of judging distances and speed of other traffic.

Leave a gap of 1 m/yd for each m.p.h. you are travelling at. For example, if you are driving at 70 m.p.h. then allow 70 metres/yards.

To gauge this distance use the 2 second rule: when the vehicle in front of you passes a fixed point (emergency phone, bridge, signpost, etc.) count 2 seconds by saying slowly: one second, two seconds. If you can say this before your vehicle reaches the fixed point then you have allowed sufficient space.
However if you cannot say 1 second, 2 seconds before reaching the same fixed point then you are following too close, so ease off on the gas and drop further back.

A very useful guideline to help you maintain your overall stopping distance at 70 m.p.h. (93m/yds) is to use the marker posts to help you.

Marker posts are to be found on the left-hand side of the hard shoulder. They are placed every 100m along the hard shoulder.
Because they are 100m/yds apart they will give you a practical way of judging the distance between yourself and other traffic.

The marker posts are there for the following reasons:

* Indicate the direction of the nearest emergency phone.

* To provide an accurate location reference in the event of accidents/ emergencies.

The numbers on the marker posts refer to the distance from the beginning of the motorway in kilometres and tenths, i.e. 36
6
Generally this will start at the London end of a motorway.
On the M25 the distance is marked in a clockwise direction from the Dartford Tunnel.

26. 11 Changing lanes

When changing to a lane on your right use the following sequence:

i)   Interior mirror;

ii)   Door mirror (driver's side);

iii)   Signal;

iv)   Door mirror (driver's side) again;

v)   Check over your right shoulder (turn your head only, no body movement as this could cause you to veer off course).

Keep the car centrally positioned and straight whilst carrying out the above.

Do not be changing lanes as you check your mirror as you signal as you check over your shoulder!

You will see cars which signal and move lanes at the same time, as though their signal gave them the right to do this! This is incorrect - plan your move giving yourself enough time for each part:

* Mirror (assess following traffic).

* Driver's door mirror (asses traffic, how fast is traffic approaching?)

* Signal (in good time).

* Driver's door mirror (again to judge speed of approaching traffic).

* Check on right shoulder (blind spot check, quick glance turning your head only - no body movement).

If safe move into new lane, mirror check for following traffic.

If you are travelling in the right-hand lane of a 3 lane motorway remember that it is for **overtaking** only, and you must move back to the left as soon as you can, without cutting in.
There is a belief amongst 'experienced' drivers that you can only stay in the outside lane for a specific time. This is not true - circumstances will dictate the amount of time you will travel in it.

As a guideline though, stay in the outside lane of a 3 lane motorway only for as long as is necessary.

Extra mirror checks are vital on motorways, especially before changing lanes. This is due to the possible high speed of traffic approaching from behind. Consider that if you are travelling at 70 m.p.h. and a vehicle coming up behind you is travelling at 120 m.p.h.. (not uncommon, the majority of motor cars are capable of 100 m.p.h. +) it will be closing on you at 50 m.p.h. (120 - 70) or 75ft/25m per second.

Checking your mirror just once would not convey to you the speed of such a vehicle. Checking 2 or 3 times would - in that time the larger the image in your mirror becomes, the faster the vehicle approaching.

This ability to judge speed and distance will come with practice, and if you become a regular user of motorways you will get 'tuned in' to travelling at higher speeds and judging the speeds of other vehicles.
This is obviously more difficult at night so take particular care.

26. 12 On the hard shoulder . . .

Use the hard shoulder only for accidents and emergencies. If you break down on the motorway, drive your car on to the hard shoulder, and where possible drive up to the nearest emergency phone. These phones are orange and white (orange and black in Scotland) and are placed to the left - hand side (grass verge side) of the hard shoulder.

These phones are:

* 1 mile apart.

* Connected to the police, who will then arrange for the AA/RAC to come to you.

* Free. No charge is made. Make sure you have all relevant details (make of car, registration number, etc., AA/RAC membership number).

* Indicated by marker posts (every 100m) on edge of hard shoulder.

Note: **Do not** cross the carriageway to use a phone.

When talking to the operator on the emergency phone be as precise and clear as possible. If you are a female travelling alone, inform the operator and they will endeavour to arrange a priority AA/RAC visit, and will ensure that a police patrol car is in the vicinity; when awaiting help lock yourself in your vehicle (sit in the passenger seat) and do not open the doors or windows if anybody approaches. Make sure your vehicle is as far to the left of the hard shoulder as possible.

To reduce the risk of your car breaking down on the motorway, ensure that it is properly maintained and that you have sufficient fuel for your journey. Remember that service stations may be far apart. Check your route beforehand and note where the service stations are.

26. 13 Motorway accidents

Although motorways are the safest roads in Great Britain (only 2% of the accidents happen on motorways) when an accident does happen it tends to involve more vehicles and appear worse than it actually is.

If you are driving past the scene of an accident, either on your carriageway or the one going the other way, **do not** 'rubberneck' (stare at it) as you drive by. Many further accidents have resulted from such behaviour. Keep your eyes on the road and concentrate on your own driving.

Many accidents on motorways involve 4 or 5 cars which have 'shunted' into each other. The leading vehicle may have braked suddenly causing following traffic to do the same thing. If an adequate gap is not left, the result is a 'concertina - crash' accident. This type of accident occurs more frequently in adverse weather conditions due to the fact that drivers do not leave sufficient clearance.

If you are involved in such an accident, and your vehicle is driveable, get it onto the hard shoulder. Obviously take particular care when driving across lanes to the hard shoulder. It is **extremely** dangerous to stay on the carriageway, discussing with other drivers the circumstances of the accident!

26. 14 Motorway service stations

The only place you can legally stop on a motorway is at a service station. They are mostly open 24 hours and offer restaurant/shop/phone/WC and fuel facilities. Motorway service stations are signposted well in advance.

Use this advance warning to make sure you are in the left-hand lane on approach. There will be count-down markers (300, 200, 100yd/m signs). Mirror check, then signal left at the

300 yd/m marker. Move into the deceleration lane to slow down sufficiently to enable you to assess the layout. Many service stations have separate lanes and parking facilities for cars/lorries/coaches. Watch out for any signs to indicate this. Also, some service stations indicate that you should fill up with petrol (if necessary) before eating: obviously the layout of the service station will dictate this and it will be clearly signposted.

Generally, at service stations you will only be able to continue on the carriageway that you have been travelling on.

Be aware that drivers may not have noticed advance signs for a service station, and could 'cut across' lanes to enter the service station.

When rejoining the motorway use the same procedure as if joining from a slip road (see 26. 9).

26. 15 The M25 . . .

The infamous M25 deserves a special mention. Because of its orbital nature, the traffic on the M25 will vary enormously, from local traffic joining for one junction, to continental traffic from the channel ports linking up with other motorways.

You are quite likely to see literally anything happening on the M25, so do not be surprised to see some strange sights . . . Do not be distracted and maintain your safety zones.

Very often the M25 is packed with all 3 (or 4) lanes full of traffic. Occasionally, and for no apparent reason, the whole carriageway comes to a complete stop. This could be for 5 minutes or 2 hours or more . . . ! If you do get stuck in such a jam, do not get out and walk around (this is illegal). Remember that motorbikes may be 'threading' their way through between vehicles, and would not take too kindly to open car doors or strolling pedestrians!

Do not ever use the hard shoulder to escape a traffic jam (emergency vehicles may need to use it), nor reverse up a slip road or cross the central reservation to do a U-turn. These manoeuvres are illegal, but above all, they are highly dangerous to other road users.
In such a traffic jam just relax and keep calm, checking mirrors for traffic movement (motorcyclists/emergency vehicles).

26. 16 Leaving a motorway

You will generally leave a motorway by an exit on the left.

Make sure that you get into the left-hand lane in good time. You will get notice of the exit from traffic signs. The first sign for an exit is 1 mile, then $\frac{1}{2}$ mile. As a guideline, at 60 mph you are travelling at one mile per minute. So at the 1 mile sign, make sure you have sufficient time to get in the left-hand lane; consider volume and speed of other traffic. As you get closer to the exit there are 'count-down' markers at 300, 200 and 100yds/m.

Mirror check, then at the 300 yard marker signal left, and then move into the deceleration lane to slow down to join the exit road.

When leaving a motorway, check your speedometer - you may be travelling faster than you think.
The new road you are joining will have different speed limits and restrictions so watch out for traffic signs and make the necessary adjustments to your driving.

When approaching exits, be aware that drivers may be crossing lanes 'at the last moment', having misjudged the distance to the exit.

26. 17 SUMMARY: dual carriageways.motorways

* Importance of lane discipline (keep left).

* Adjusting to higher speeds.

* Allowing a safety gap (1m/yd per m.p.h.)

* Adjustment of speed when leaving a motorway.

27

ADVANCED DRIVING

27.1 What is advanced driving?

Firstly, to dispel some popular beliefs.
It is **not:**

* Driving everywhere at high speed.

* Screeching around corners.

* Doing handbrake turns.

Advanced driving can be summed up as:

The driver being in total harmony with his vehicle, being in the appropriate gear and at the correct speed for any and all given situations, whilst making brisk progress in complete safety with due regard for all other road users, and complying with speed limits, road traffic and weather conditions. An advanced driver will plan ahead and assess all hazards, and act accordingly, to allow the maximum possible safety margin at all times.
He will not put himself or other road users in a situation which is potentially or actually dangerous.

27.2 'O' and 'A' level driving ...

Look upon passing your driving test as an 'O' level in driving.
You have demonstrated that you have

shown a basic competence to drive.

Advanced driving is the 'A' level version, with your driving being more skilful, smooth and flowing.

As with all areas of education, driving can be taken to a higher level, and the highest level open to civilian drivers is the R.o.S.P.A. Diploma in Advanced Driving Techniques.

Benefits from being an advanced driver are:

* Reduced insurance premiums.

* Improved safety awareness.

* Greater enjoyment from your driving.

* Reduced wear and tear on your vehicle.

* Saving money on repairs and maintenance.

* Personal achievement.

It is advisable that new drivers should have some experience, say 18 months - 2 years or 20,000 miles of various types of driving before taking an advanced driving test.

The reason for this is so that you can gain a greater appreciation of all the tasks involved in driving in various conditions and on different roads.

Advanced driving is taught using a particular 'system' to approach and deal with hazards.

This system has been developed and refined over many years and is well proven as a safe and correct method of driving. All police drivers are taught to drive this way.

To understand this 'system' it is recommended that you seek advice from an instructor who has a knowledge of, and understanding of, the 'system of car control'.

27. 3 Advanced Instructors . . .

There are instructors who advertise that they teach 'advanced driving', but in reality have very little grasp of the concept or application of it themselves.

When choosing an instructor for advanced driving, check first of all that they are qualified and have passed one or both of the advanced driving tests. Ask them when they took their last advanced test and if they can explain it in a little more detail.

Remember that anyone giving driving tuition for payment (or monies worth) must be an approved driving instructor (A.D.I.)

Just being an advanced driver does not entitle that person to give tuition for payment.

There are two organisations that administer and carry out advanced driving tests:

*   (I. A. M.) The Institute of Advanced Motorists.

*   (R. o. S. P. A.) The Royal Society for the Prevention of Accidents. Advanced Drivers Association.

Both of these organisations are registered charities whose aim is to promote road safety, and to drive with care, consideration and courtesy.

The way that each organisation administers the tests, what is involved, etc., will now be covered in detail.

27. 4 The advanced driving test - what is it?

The test itself will consist of a drive of approximately 1 hour 20 minutes over a variety of roads, urban, rural, motorway (if practical) dual carriageways in varying traffic conditions.

You will be expected to drive to a high standard, and to the 'system', as previously mentioned. You will comply with all traffic signs and road markings.

You will be asked to carry out one or more manoeuvring exercises.

You will be invited to give a commentary as you drive. This is optional and you may decline to do this; if so it will not adversely affect the result of the test.

You will also be expected to demonstrate a practical and theoretical knowledge of the Highway Code.

At the end of the test you will be told the result and given a 'debriefing' in which the examiner will comment on your driving and advise on any area to which you should pay particular attention.

The advanced driving test is less formal and rigid than the 'L' test in that the candidate may speak to the examiner and pass comment. However, the examiner will not generally engage in, or initiate, conversation not connected with driving.

27. 5   Who are the examiners?

The examiners for both organisations are all serving or ex-Police traffic patrol officers. They are very experienced drivers themselves and they all hold Police class 1 driving certificates. To achieve this, Police drivers have attended an intensive 6 week advanced driving course, and must then pass a rigorous assessment with a very high pass mark.

Class 1 police drivers can be rightly regarded as the most highly trained and expert of all drivers in either the police or civilian field.

Those examiners who are serving Police officers have special dispensation from their chief constables to act as advanced driving test examiners. They give their time voluntarily, in the interest of furthering road safety.

All of the examiners are approachable and will try to ensure a relaxed and informal atmosphere. They will not wear uniforms!

27. 6 Who, what, when and where

R.o.S.P.A.
  Advanced Drivers Association.
  Cannon House.
  Priory Queensway.
  Birmingham B4 6BS.
  021-200-2461
  (ask for Advanced Drivers
                        Association)

R.o.S.P.A. conduct advanced driving tests throughout the UK, and will arrange a test on a day and time that is mutually convenient for you and your examiner. The test will be conducted in daylight where possible.

Generally you should be able to take a test within 3 weeks of applying. This may vary though, according to the availability of the examiner.

R.o.S.P.A. advanced driving tests are graded 1, 2, 3. Grade 1 is the highest grade. A free refresher test is taken every 3 years to ensure that the standard of your driving is maintained or improved if necessary.

Grade 1 drivers can apply to take a diploma in advanced driving techniques consisting of written, practical and instructional tests.

Facts about the R.o.S.P.A. advanced driving test:

You will need to show your driving licence, M.O.T. (where applicable) and insurance certificate.

Duration: 1 $\frac{1}{4}$ hours plus debriefing afterwards.

Manoeuvres: Left -hand reverse.

Written Report: Yes, very detailed on all aspects of the drive.

Fee: £24.95 (This includes the first year's annual subscription).

Result: Will be given at end of test, with fully detailed written report approximately 2 weeks later. Certificate sent within 3 weeks.

Commentary: Preferred but not compulsory. Highway Code questions will be asked.

The annual subscription entitles you to receive the R.o.S.P.A. magazine 'Care on the Road' bi-monthly which covers all aspects of road safety, along with car reviews, etc.

R.o.S.P.A. have 300 examiners throughout the UK.

There are 35 local groups which meet regularly to discuss all aspects of road safety, and also as social occasions.

These local groups can advise you as to the exact requirements of the test, and members can also act as 'observers' to assess your driving.

On an 'observed run' a member of the Advanced Drivers' Association would accompany you on a drive over a varied route, taking the items into consideration that examiners have regard to when testing you. Although there is no charge for these 'observed runs', an associate membership fee may be payable to the local group.

After the 'observed run' the observer will give you a verbal and/or written debriefing of your drive, drawing your attention to items to which you should pay particular note.

It is advisable to then practice improving your driving to the necessary standard. Further observed runs will confirm any improvements and the observer can advise you as to when to apply for the test.

It is unlikely that any driver would pass an advanced driving test without prior assessment, advice or tuition.

Be prepared to accept that your driving may require some adjustments to reach the necessary high standard, and treat any advice given as positive and constructive.

27. 7 The Institute of Advanced Motorists

The Institute of Advanced Motorists
I.A.M.
359 Chiswick High Road
London W4 4HS
081-994-4403

The I.A.M. also conduct advanced driving tests throughout the UK. Generally you will be given 3 weeks notice of a test, and the timing will be mutually convenient for you and the examiner.

I.A.M. tests are pass or fail, and not graded. Although refresher tests are not taken as a matter of course, it is possible to take a voluntary re-test (for a fee) as and when a driver feels it to be necessary.

The I.A.M. do not operate a diploma course.

Facts about the Institute of Advanced Motorists driving test:

You will need to show your driving licence, M.O.T. (where applicable) and insurance certificate.

Duration: 1¹/₂ hours drive (approx.) prior briefing 10-15 minutes and then debriefing afterwards for as long as necessary.

Manoeuvres: Left or right hand reverse, turn-in-the-road, reverse parallel park (between 2 cars).

Written Report:
No. Candidates who fail will get a pre-printed report form with items marked that led to an unsuccessful test result.

Fee: £30.00 (This includes the first year's annual subscription).

Result: Will be given at the end of the test. If you pass you will receive a certificate within approximately 3 weeks.

Commentary: I.A.M. do not insist on it. If you do not give a commentary the examiner will generally ask you to "identify the last road sign", or to mention the traffic signs as you see them, along with their meaning. Apart from this, no specific Highway Code questions will be asked.

The annual subscription entitles you to receive the I.A.M. magazine 'Milestones' 3 times per year. This magazine covers various current motoring matters, together with car reviews, readers letters, discounts, on motoring services and advertising for motoring and general interests.

The I.A.M. have 270 examiners throughout the UK.

There are 180 local groups which meet regularly to discuss all aspects of road safety and also as social occasions.

These local groups can advise you as to the exact requirements of the test, and members can also act as 'observers' to assess your driving.

On such an 'observed run' a member of the Institute of Advanced Drivers would accompany you on a drive over a varied route, taking the items into consideration that examiners have regard of when testing you. Although there is no charge for these 'observed runs', an associate membership fee may be payable to the local group.

After the 'observed run' the observer will give you a verbal and/or written debriefing of your drive, drawing your attention to items which you should particularly note.

It is then advisable to practice improving your driving to the necessary standard.
Further 'observed runs' will then confirm any improvements, and the observer can advise you as to when to apply for the test.

It is unlikely that any driver would pass an advanced driving test without proper assessment advice or tuition.

Be prepared to accept that your driving may require some adjustments to reach the necessary high standard, and treat any advice given as positive and constructive.

27. 8 Company car drivers

Both R.o.S.P.A. the I.A.M. and the R.A.C. operate fleet training schemes on a commercial basis for companies operating fleets of vehicles.

These course are designed to improve safety awareness, develop the skills of company car drivers and reduce fleet running costs.

Vehicles driven with consideration and 'car sympathy' will require less maintenance, therefore reducing running costs.

Drivers with heightened awareness and the right attitude to driving will have fewer accidents - therefore reducing the time off the road through injury, administration, etc., and savings on repair bills, hire cars, etc.

It should be noted that a significant number of company cars are not insured fully comprehensively because of the high cost of doing so. Any damage to the vehicle must therefore be borne by the fleet operator. It follows therefore that any increase in the running costs of a company will ultimately be passed on to the consumer - meaning higher prices in the shops.

27. 9 SUMMARY: advanced driving

* Driving to a 'system'.

* Safety at all times.

* Planning well ahead.

* Hazard recognition.

* R.o.S.P.A. and I.A.M.

* Company car drivers.

28

MECHANICAL KNOWLEDGE, M. O. T., ETC.

28. 1 Safety related mechanics

Although it is not necessary to know how a car works in order to drive it, it is essential that you are able to identify basic vehicle defects that will affect the safety of your vehicle.

28. 2 What is the 'M.O.T.' ?

It is a way of ensuring all vehicles are roadworthy to certain standards. Usually referred to as the 'M.O.T.' it is a Ministry of Transport certificate of roadworthiness. It is a legal requirement that all vehicles over 3 years old must have an annual inspection at an approved vehicle testing station (outside which the prescribed sign must be exhibited). If this inspection is satisfactory, the vehicle will be issued with an M.O.T. certificate (an A5 document), with details of the vehicle: make, registration number, mileage etc. It should be borne in mind though, that such a certificate is only 'good on the day', and when considering buying a vehicle do not assume that all is well just because it has an M.O.T. certificate.

The items that are checked at an M.O.T. inspection are all safety related and are:

> Brakes
> Steering
> Lights
> Reflectors
> Stop lamps
> Tyres
> Wheels
> Seat-belts and anchorages
> Direction indicators
> Windscreen wipers/washers
> Exhaust system/emissions
> Warning instruments
> Bodywork/suspension

An M.O.T. inspection will usually take under 1 hour and currently costs £15.50.

Yellow Pages will list approved testing stations. You may need to book your vehicle in, or it could be done while you wait.

You will need a valid M.O.T. certificate to tax your vehicle (if it is over 3 years old).

Keep your M.O.T. certificate in a safe place (not in the car) with other car documents so that, if necessary, they can be located as and when required. The M.O.T. certificate is valid for 12 months.

28. 3 Recognising defects

Once you have recognised a defect, you should rectify it as soon as possible. If you are unable to do this yourself you will need to enlist qualified help. Ask around family or friends to see if they can recommend a garage or mechanic, or look in Yellow Pages for a specific item, i.e. exhaust centre, tyre fitter, etc.
Although vehicles could have many faults, the basic safety related ones are listed here:

28. 4 Steering

When the vehicle is driven on a straight course, with the steering wheel held lightly, does it veer from side to side? (When doing this avoid white lines which can 'pull' the car one way or the other; white -lining).
Does the steering have a vague feel to it?
Does it make noises when turning the wheel (clonks, rattles, etc.)?
Does the car follow the course you are steering, or does it drift off line?

If any of the above occur it could indicate a defect in the steering system and related components. Seek advice.

28. 5 Brakes

When braking, does the car pull to one side or the other?
Do the brakes judder/ (Not applicable to A.B.S.)
Is there a grinding noise when you brake?

Does the brake pedal feel spongy? (A lot of travel but no significant response.) Are the brake warning lights on? Is there a smell of burning from any of the wheels?

If any of the above occur, it could indicate a defect in the braking system. Seek advice.

28. 6 Tyres

It is important that tyres are kept at the correct pressure (see your vehicle's handbook) for the use and loading. Tyres which are under or over-inflated can cause problems with the steering and handling of the car, and cause excessive or uneven tyre wear.

Check tyre pressure once a week, at the same air-line if possible. This is because different air-lines may give slightly different readings. Always check your tyre pressures when cold. After a long journey the tyre will heat up, expanding the air inside to give a higher reading which could be misleading.

The minimum tread depth requirement is:

* 1mm on $^3/_4$ tyre width and all around circumference.

* Visible tread pattern on remaining $^1/_4$ of tyre.

* Bald or worn patches are illegal.

Visibly check all tyres for cuts, bulges, etc., or nails, pieces of metal sticking in them.

Uneven tyre wear (i.e. inner or outer shoulder wearing, etc.) can indicate that the 'tracking' is out.

If you have any doubts about the legality of your tyres, get a tyre fitter to check them for you.

Do not forget to check the spare tyre. It must be legal and correctly inflated (if your front and rear tyres have different pressures, then set the spare at the higher pressure - you can always reduce it if necessary).

The tyres which are on the driven wheels will wear more quickly. Consider changing then around to balance out the wear. Harsh acceleration and braking can dramatically reduce the life of your tyres, as can scraping against, or driving up, kerbs.

Remember, the tyres are your contact with the road, so look after them!

28 .7 Seat-belts

If your seat-belts are the inertia reel type (allowing freedom of movement) check each time you put it on that it locks. Do this by gripping the belt with your right hand and giving a sharp tug. The belt should then lock.
Are the seat-belts worn or frayed? If so, replace them.
If the car has been involved in an accident the seat-belts and anchorage points will have taken a great deal of strain and may need replacing. Seek advice.

Also check rear seat-belts, if fitted. If they are not fitted, consider having them installed. In the event of an impact it will prevent your rear seat passengers from flying around!

28. 8 Lights

All lights must be clean and in good working order. A regular check should be made (walk around the car) to make sure that all bulbs are working correctly.
Some cars have an in-built dashboard display to show where a bulb is inoperative. There are also inexpensive accessory kits that can be bought to provide a similar system. This is achieved by using fibre-optics which attach to each light lens and then to the instrument panel.

Different vehicles use different bulbs, and replacement kits can be bought which contain one of each type.
Your vehicle's handbook will show you how to change a bulb; or seek advice.

Headlights must be correctly aligned and matched, be capable of being dipped, and both show the same colour (white or yellow).

28. 9 Reflectors

You must have 2 red reflectors facing to the rear of (one on each side) your vehicle.
Generally these are included in the light cluster. Their purpose is to reflect light back from approaching vehicles, making them aware of your vehicle (especially when parked at night).

These reflectors must be kept clean and be plainly visible from the rear, unobscured and effective.

28.10 Direction Indicators

Direction indicators must be kept in good working order.

There is a warning light or audible signal (clicking) inside the car to show that the indicators are working.
Regularly check that all bulbs are working by getting out of the car, or asking someone else to, and check each indicator.
Usually if a bulb fails on one side, the indicator will 'flash' more quickly on the other side.

If your direction indicators do fail completely, first check the fuse box, it could be that a fuse has blown.
The purpose of a fuse is to prevent the whole electrical system failing as a result of just one item. There can be up to 10 circuits in a car which are protected by fuses.
The vehicle's handbook will identify these.
Having found the relevant fuse, a visual check will tell you if it has 'blown'. The fuse consists of a piece of wire in a container (plastic/ceramic) of some sort. If the wire is broken then the fuse has blown and will need to be replaced. Keep a supply of fuses in the car as a back-up, if required. If, on replacing the fuse, it blows again then it will be necessary to seek advice.
An electrical problem can be difficult to trace - there are literally hundreds of metres of wiring in a car!

If your direction indicators fail, you will need to use arm signals, see chapter 6. 7

28.11 Windscreen wipers and washers

If the wipers or washers suddenly fail to work, check the fuses (see 28.10).

The wipers must effectively clear the screen. If any areas are left unswept or smeared, consider replacing the wiper blades. Obviously visibility is paramount to safety so make sure you can see at all times. Wiper blades are relatively inexpensive and should be replaced every year. Greasy deposits can build up on the blades, and if not cleaned off will be smeared back on the screen.

Screen washers must be working efficiently. If no water is coming out of the nozzles first check that the water reservoir is full. It it is and there is still no water coming out of the nozzles check the tubing from the reservoir to the valve or nozzles.

28.12 Horn

All vehicles must be fitted with an instrument capable of giving audible warning of approach. The sound given must be continuous, uniform and not strident.

If your horn is inoperative, or is working erratically it would indicate that a wiring connection may be faulty. Most horn units are situated at the front of the engine compartment and are therefore exposed to the elements which can cause corrosion of the terminals resulting in total or partial inoperation. If this is the case, seek advice (auto/electrician).

28. 13 Rear view mirrors

Make sure all mirrors are secure (not flapping about or hanging off) and properly adjusted. Many interior mirrors are secured to the windscreen with a double-sided sticky pad. Eventually this could lose its grip, causing the interior mirror to drop off, or be pulled off when adjusting. Spare double-sided pads can be bought at accessory shops for a few pence. Keep a couple in the car. Extreme weather changes could cause the pad to lose its adhesion.

In the case of a motor vehicle first used on or after 1st April 1969 the edges of an internally fitted mirror must be surrounded by some material such as will render the edges and surface unlikely to cause severe cuts if the mirror or material is struck by an occupant of the vehicle.

28. 14 Speedometer

Must be able to be easily read by the driver, and free from any obstructions which might prevent that. It must be in good working order, accurate to within 10%. If the needle is fluctuating wildly, or stuck at a certain speed or not operating at all it indicates a fault with the speedometer cable and will need professional attention.

28. 15 Exhaust system

Must be in good working order and effective, not causing excessive noise, and must be properly secured. All exhaust gases must pass through the silencer.

If you notice excessive noise from the exhaust system (it might sound like a tractor) this is usually caused by a hole or crack in the exhaust system. Any noise will be much louder when the engine is cold, When it heats up the metal will expand to seal a crack or hole, possibly completely. However, do not ignore it, the damage will get worse and worse. At the first sign of such a problem take the car to an exhaust centre (try Yellow Pages) where they will put it up on a ramp for inspection and rectification. It may just be that bolts have come loose, or alternatively it could be a corroded system.

Also, visibly check the exhaust system by looking underneath the car. You do not necessarily have to crawl underneath but stand about 10m/yds behind the car, crouch down and look to see if any part of the exhaust system is hanging down or loose.

If there is a loud 'clonking' sound when you start the engine or move off on a hill, it could indicate that a restraining strap has broken and the exhaust is knocking against the underside of the car.

28.16 Wheels

Check the physical condition of the wheels for dents, buckles, etc.

If the wheels are out of 'balance', you will feel vibration/shuddering through the steering wheel at certain speeds. This can be rectified by a tyre fitting centre who have the necessary equipment.
It should be noted that on front wheel drive cars it may be necessary to have the front wheels balanced on the car, to satisfactorily eliminate any imbalance.

When having wheels balanced also get the 'tracking' checked. This is the degree of 'lean' that all wheels have, either leaning in or out. A tyre fitting centre will have all manufacturers' specifications and the necessary equipment to check it.

28.17 Changing a wheel

If you have a puncture, or want to change wheels around, it should be done in this order:

* Ensure vehicle handbrake is on, and the vehicle is on firm level ground.

* Remove spare wheel, jack and wheel-brace from stowage location.

* Remove wheel-trim on the wheel you are changing.
  (Note that on some vehicles there are plastic nut shaped covers over the wheel nuts. These plastic covers need to be removed!)

* Using the wheel-brace, slacken the wheel nuts by turning them half a turn anti-clockwise. Do not remove the wheel nuts.

* Consult your vehicle's handbook as to where the jacking points are. Slide the jack arm into the jacking point nearest the corner of the vehicle which is to be raised.

* Jack the vehicle up, by turning the handle clockwise until the wheel is clear of the ground (only 1"/2.5cm clearance is necessary).

* Using the wheel-brace, remove all the wheel nuts and then remove the wheel from the vehicle.

* Fit the spare wheel and replace the wheel nuts. Tighten the wheel nuts in a clockwise direction using the wheel-brace.

* Lower the vehicle to the ground by turning the handle of the jack anti-clockwise. Keep turning until the jack is free of the vehicle.

* Fully tighten the wheel nuts. Do this diagonally - tighten one, then the one diagonally opposite, and so on.

* Finally, check each wheel nut again, making sure they have been tightened as much as possible.

* Replace any wheel trim - ensure it is correctly aligned over the valve, etc.

Note: If, unavoidably, you have to change a wheel on soft ground, try to 'spread the load' by placing a piece of wood, hard-back book, etc., under the foot of the jack. If this is not done the jack will sink into the ground and the vehicle will not be raised.

28.18 SUMMARY: mechanical knowledge, M.O.T., etc.

* Routine safety checks.

* Identify defects.

* The M.O.T.

* Changing a wheel.

29

FAULT CORRECTOR

29.1 There are certain basic faults which are committed by learner drivers. All other faults are variations of these.

The following table has been compiled to enable you to identify a particular fault and its probable cause.

29.2 MOVING AWAY UNDER CONTROL

Fault	Cause
Car 'kangaroo' jumping when moving away or stalling	Not co-ordinating the clutch with the gas pedal Clutch pedal coming up too quickly, not enough gas. (Another cause could be incorrect footwear).
Car rolling backwards (on up-hill starts)	Clutch pedal not at biting point before handbrake released.
Car moving away too quickly (on down hill starts)	Incorrect technique being used (uphill instead of downhill).
Car getting too close to other vehicles in angled start	Either driving too quickly or not steering quickly enough, or a combination of both.

29.3 MOVING AWAY SAFELY

Fault	Cause
Moving away without checking blind spot properly, possibly causing traffic approaching from behind to swerve or slow down to avoid you.	Not checking over your shoulder before the car moves. This must be done every time, even if you are only driving the car forward 1m/yd.

29. 4   POSITIONING

Fault	Cause
Driving too close to the kerb/parked cars. Driving too close to the middle of the road.	Not being aware of your vehicles position in relation to the kerb/parked cars, or other moving traffic.
Being incorrectly positioned when the road narrows (either physically or due to parked vehicles/obstructions).	Not being aware of situations developing. Not reading the road ahead and anticipating what could happen, and taking the necessary action.

29. 5   MAKING NORMAL STOPS

Fault	Cause
When stopping, the car 'jolts' (making occupants jerk forward).	Not braking progressively. See page 30.
Stopping in an unsafe place.	Not being aware of surroundings - obstructions, parked vehicles, driveways etc.
Stopping too far from the kerb. Stopping too close to the kerb; scraping or scuffing wheels/tyres on the kerb.	Not being aware of your vehicles width, and also the position of the nearside (passenger) wheels in relation to the kerb.

29. 6   USE OF THE GEARS

Fault	Cause
Gears not going in properly or 'crunching'.	Clutch pedal not pressed down (fully). Incorrect hand position on gear lever.
Car shuddering or 'labouring'.	Not selecting the correct gear to match the speed of the car. Wrong gear selected (i.e. 4th instead of 2nd etc.).
Car 'jolts' when selecting a lower gear, causing car to suddenly slow down.	Lower gear selected too early, without the speed having been sufficiently reduced by the brake.
Engine 'roaring' or sounding too loud.	Not selecting a higher gear earlier (i.e. driving in 1st gear when you should have changed to 2nd gear).

29. 7 STEERING

Fault	Cause
Veering towards kerb/parked vehicles, or drifting toward centre of road.	Not looking far enough ahead. Do not look at kerb or parked vehicles, but look as far ahead as you can and also scan both sides of the road. Another cause could be taking your eyes off the road to look at the speedometer or the gear lever. Gripping the steering wheel too tightly will also cause this. Hold the steering wheel lightly, as though you are holding eggs.
Going too wide when turning.	Not using large enough movements of the steering wheel. Use the pull-push method as described on page 25. Also make sure you are sitting in such a position that you can operate the steering wheel effectively, safely and under control at all times.

29. 8 APPROACHING AND TURNING CORNERS

Fault	Cause
Approaching too quickly.	Not braking sufficiently , or coasting (clutch pedal held down) on approach.
When turning, going over onto the wrong side of the road.	Speed too high at point-of-turn. Inadequate braking on approach or coasting (clutch held down) when turning. Another cause could be insufficient steering at point-of-turn, or turning too late.
Veering in or out on approach to the corner.	Not keeping the car at a constant distance from the left hand kerb.
Cutting right hand corners.	Not turning at the correct point-of-turn. Turning too early.

DRIVING TOO FAST/TOO SLOWLY

Fault	Cause
Exceeding the speed limit.	Nor judging the speed of your vehicle correctly. Not being aware of changing speed limits.
Driving too fast for road/traffic/weather conditions, not slowing down or being prepared to slow down for hazards.	Not being aware of hazards, not recognising hazards and considering what could happen.
Driving too closely behind other road users.	Not being aware of your stopping distance (or not being able to judge those distances when driving).
Driving too slowly.	Not judging the speed of your vehicle. Not being aware of changing speed limits, road conditions etc. Not keeping up with the traffic flow. Taking too long to build up speed between gear changes. Reducing speed too early for turnings.
Being too hesitant at junctions.	Not having the car prepared and ready to emerge (gas set, clutch just below biting point, hand on handbrake). Not judging speed or distance of approaching traffic.

29. 10 THE EMERGENCY STOP

Fault	Cause
Not stopping promptly enough.	Not reacting quickly enough, not alert or aware of situation. Not braking firmly enough. Pushing clutch pedal down too early. (The car will take longer to stop).
Locking the wheels (wheels stop turning) - car slides or skids along the road.	Stamping on the footbrake. Not being ware of the different road surfaces and their effect on braking distances. Not being aware of the correct action to take if the wheels do lock.
Having stopped, not checking over both shoulders before moving away.	Not being aware that road users could be driving/riding up on both sides. (You might be stopped in the middle of the road).

29. 11 TURN-IN-THE-ROAD

Fault	Cause
Taking too many turns to complete the manoeuvre.	Not turning the steering wheel quickly enough. Driving the vehicle too quickly. Not parking close enough to the kerb when first starting the manoeuvre.
Driving into the kerb.	Not being aware of your vehicles length or the position of the wheels in relation to the kerb.
Rolling forward (or backwards) into the kerb.	Not finding the biting point before releasing the handbrake.
Stalling	Insufficient control of clutch/gas. Not enough gas.

Fault	Cause
Driving into kerb.	Not controlling the vehicle sufficiently. Not being aware of your vehicles position in relation to the kerb.
'Clipping' or mounting the kerb when reversing around the corner.	Not turning at the correct point-of-turn; turning too early.
Going too wide when reversing.	Not turning at the correct point-of-turn; turning too late.
Steering the wrong way.	Not looking backwards when steering. Remember, always look the way you are going and steer the way you want the car to go.
'Weaving' along the road.	Steering too much one way, then over-correcting.
Reversing too quickly.	Not realising that the slower you go, the more time you will have to steer, observe and correct any errors.

29.13 PARALLEL PARKING CLOSE TO THE KERB USING REVERSE GEAR

Fault	Cause
Reversing into the gap at too sharp an angle.	Turning the steering wheel too far to the left at the point-of-turn.
Reversing into the gap at too shallow an angle.	Not steering sufficiently at the point-of-turn.
Pulling up too close to the vehicle behind which you intend to park.	Not allowing sufficient clearance (ideally 1m/3ft).
Excessive backward and forward movements to position vehicle squarely in gap.	Either too high a speed for the manoeuvre, or not large enough movements of the steering wheel, or a combination of both.
Not being able to park in the available space.	Misjudgement of space required for your vehicle. Minimum requirement is a gap of 1 $\frac{1}{2}$ - 2 vehicle lengths. A larger gap will be required when parking on a slope